6018

2005 08 12

D0207506

NIAGARA COLLEGE

LEARNING RESOURCE CENTRE

Glendale Campus

OVERDUE CHARGES
$.25 PER DAY

SIMULATION MODELLING FOR BUSINESS

Innovative Business Textbooks

The purpose of this series is to provide business textbooks for specialist, option or advanced courses. Published in hardback at paperback prices and written by acknowledged experts, Innovative Business Textbooks are comprehensive and reliable. Each includes a range of learning aids to assist both lecturer and student.

Other titles in the series

Simulation Modelling for Business

200201

ANDREW GREASLEY
Aston Business School, UK

ASHGATE

Published by
Ashgate Publishing Limited
Gower House
Croft Road
Aldershot
Hants GU11 3HR
England

Ashgate Publishing Company
Suite 420
101 Cherry Street
Burlington, VT 05401-4405
USA

Ashgate website: http://www.ashgate.com

British Library Cataloguing in Publication Data
Greasley, Andrew
    Simulation modelling for business. - (Innovative business
    textbooks)
    1. Business - Computer simulation 2. Management - Computer
    simulation 3. Decision making - Computer simulation
    4. Decision support systems
    I. Title
    658.4'0352

Library of Congress Cataloging-in-Publication Data
Greasley, Andrew.
  Simulation modelling for business / Andrew Greasley.
      p. cm. -- (Innovative business textbooks)
  Includes bibliographical references and index.
  ISBN 0-7546-3214-8
  1. Management--Simulation methods. I. Title. II. Series.

  HD30.26.G74 2003
  658'.001'1--dc22

                                                          2003045232

  ISBN 0 7546 3214 8

Printed and bound in Great Britain by MPG Books Ltd, Bodmin, Cornwall

Contents

Preface

Among the reasons for the use of the simulation technique in recent years are the development of visual interactive modelling systems and the role of simulation in analysing service organisations. Visual interactive modelling systems enable the user to quickly construct simple simulation models by placing icons on a screen and then connecting them together to represent the process flow of a system. This method of simulation construction is in contrast to the former method of writing a computer program in a simulation language. Simulation has also found a role in many business process re-engineering and process-based change methods that analyse the performance of service systems. Both these developments have helped to move simulation from a specialist industrial engineering tool to a mainstream business management technique.

In response to these developments many business and management undergraduate and postgraduate degrees now contain a simulation modelling element. From a student viewpoint this can be a stimulating and exciting development. Firstly it allows the use of many of the skills previously taught including data collection methods, statistical techniques and operations management concepts. Secondly it allows for the analysis of the performance over time of real (or case study based) organisations and the presentation of recommendations for action. Specifically, simulation demonstrates the importance of the concepts of variability and interdependence on the performance of manufacturing and service organisations.

This book aims to provide a practical guide to building a simulation model. All the steps in a typical simulation study are covered including data collection, input data modelling and experimentation. A feature of the text is a guide to building a simple model using three popular and modern visual interactive modelling systems. The book also emphasises the need to understand the business context in which the simulation study will take place.

The author would welcome any comments regarding this text to a.greasley@aston.ac.uk.

Acknowledgements

I would like to thank Brendan George, the team at Ashgate Publishing Limited, and the reviewers for their support in the production of this text. Thanks to the simulation clients I have worked with over the past 15 years, including Stuart Barlow and David Smith. Thanks to Duncan Shaw for his contribution to chapter 10 and finally I would also like to thank Meamy and Philly for their very useful assistance.

This book is dedicated to Kay.

Biography

Andrew Greasley is a lecturer in the Operations and Information Management Group, Aston Business School, Aston University, Birmingham, UK. He has 15 years' experience of building simulation models for clients in the public and private sectors, including ABB, Rolls Royce, Golden Wonder and Derbyshire Constabulary. He has taught modelling techniques for a number of years in Europe and Africa, including in the UK, France, Hungary, Malawi and Zimbabwe. He has published a number of papers on simulation topics in journals such as *SIMULATION*, *Journal of the Operational Research Society*, *International Journal of Operations and Production Management*, *Quality and Reliability Engineering International* and *Business Process Management Journal*. He has authored the text book *Operations Management in Business*, published by Nelson Thornes Limited and is co-author of the text *Business Information Systems: Technology, Development and Management for the e-business* (2nd edition), published by Pearson Education Limited. He can be contacted at a.greasley@aston.ac.uk.

Chapter 1

Introduction to Simulation Modelling

Introduction

Organisational systems can be seen as a number of interconnected processes. Therefore in order to improve the performance of an organisation it is necessary to study the design of these processes and the resources that they consume. Simulation provides a way of experimenting with a model (i.e. simplified representation) of an organisational system in order to understand its behaviour under a number of scenarios. The construction of the model is thus designed to provide decision-makers with detailed information on how processes behave. This understanding will assist in making decisions which increase performance whilst minimising problems from unforeseen side effects of change.

Simulation has been used for many years in manufacturing as part of the toolkit of the industrial engineer. It has been an important element in a business context where global competitive pressures have forced manufacturers to develop increasingly efficient and effective process designs. With the advent of approaches to change such as *Business Process Re-engineering (BPR)* the idea of a process perspective to design in service applications has become widespread. With the development of more sophisticated simulation software incorporating interaction and animation effects the potential for simulation modelling as a tool for process improvement in all types of organisations is now being recognised. The main barrier to further use is the variety of skills needed in terms of project management, data collection, statistical analysis and model development to produce a useful model for decision-making. This text aims to provide a guide to the implementation of these skills.

What is Simulation Modelling?

Simulation is used to mean a number of things from a physical prototype to a video game. As it is used in this text, simulation refers to the use of a model to investigate the behaviour of a business system. The use of a model on a computer to mimic the operation of a business means that the performance of the business over an extended time period can be observed quickly and under a number of different scenarios. The simulation method usually refers to both the process of building a model and the conducting of experiments on that model. An experiment consists of repeatedly running the simulation for a time period in order to provide data for statistical analysis. An experiment is conducted in order to understand the behaviour of the model and to evaluate the effect of different input levels on specified performance measures. Pidd (2003:233) characterises systems best suited to simulation as:

- *Dynamic* Their behaviour varies over time.
- *Interactive* They consist of a number of components which interact with each other.
- *Complicated* The systems consist of many interacting and dynamic objects.

Most organisational systems have these characteristics and thus simulation would seem to be an ideal tool for providing information on the behaviour of an organisation. In practice simulation is most widely used and appropriate for applications which involve queuing – of people, materials or information. By simply defining in the simulation the timing of arrival to the queue and the availability of the resource that is being queued for, then the simulation is able to provide performance statistics on the average time in the queue and the average queue size for a particular system. A simple example would be to determine the performance of a supermarket checkout system. From information provided on customer arrival rates and checkout service times the simulation would be able to report performance measures such as average customer queue times and the utilisation of the checkout resource. Queuing systems are prevalent and examples include raw material waiting for processing in a manufacturing plant, vehicle queuing in transportation systems, documents waiting for processing in a workflow system, patients waiting to be seen in a doctor's surgery and many others.

Defining Simulation

Simulation in general covers a large area of interest and in order to clarify the particular area of interest in this text a short explanation is given of common terms in this area. Simulation can refer to a range of model types from spreadsheet models, system dynamic simulations and discrete-event simulation. *Discrete-Event Simulation* or *Simulation Modelling* is the subject of this text. Early simulation systems generated reports of system performance, but advances in software and hardware allowed the development of animation capabilities. When combined with the ability to interact with the model this technique became known as *Visual Interactive Simulation (VIS)*. Most simulation modelling software is now implemented using graphical user interfaces employing objects or icons that are placed on the screen to produce a model. These are often referred to as *Visual*

Interactive Modelling (VIM) systems. The software packages used in this text are VIMs that use the discrete-event method of operation. Finally because of the use of simulation in the context of business process re-engineering (BPR) and of other process-based change methods the technique is also referred to as *Business Process Simulation (BPS)*. The term *Business Process Modelling (BPM)* is also sometimes used, but this term is traditionally related to information system development tools.

Why Use Simulation?

Simulation modelling is used to assist decision-making by providing a tool that allows the current behaviour of a system to be analysed and understood. It is also able to help predict the performance of that system under a number of scenarios determined by the decision-maker. Simulation modelling is useful in providing the following assistance to the process improvement effort:

- *Allows Prediction* Predicts business system performance under a range of scenarios.
- *Stimulates Creativity* Helps creativity by allowing many different decision options to be tried quickly and cheaply.
- *Avoids Disruption* Allows an evaluation of a number of decision options without disruption or use of a real system.
- *Reduces Risk* Allows the evaluation of a number of possible scenario outcomes, permitting contingencies to be formulated for these outcomes and therefore reducing the risk of failure.
- *Provides Performance Measures* Can be integrated into performance measurement systems to provide organisational performance measures and cost estimates.
- *Acts as a Communication Tool* The results and computer animation can provide a forum for understanding the system behaviour. The dynamics of a system can be visualised over time, aiding understanding of system interactions.
- *Assists Acceptance of Change* Individuals can predict the effects of change, thus allowing them to accept and understand change and improve confidence towards implementation.
- *Encourages Data Collection* The systematic collection of data from a variety of sources necessary to build the model, can in itself lead to new insights on the operation of the system, before the model has been built or experimentation begun.

- *Allows Overview of Whole Process Performance* Using simulation to model processes across departmental boundaries allows improvement of the whole process, rather than the optimisation of local activities at the expense of overall performance.
- *Acts as a Training Tool* Allows personnel to be trained or provides a demonstration of process behaviour without the possible cost and disruption to the real system.
- *Acts as a Design Aid* Allows process behaviour to be observed and thus optimised at an early stage in the process design effort.

Disadvantages of the Simulation Method

Although simulation can be applied widely in the organisation, a model developed for a non-trivial problem will consume a significant amount of resource in terms of staff time. Both time and cost elements need to be considered. Thus an assessment must be made of costs against potential benefits. As with many investment decisions, however, the costs are usually substantially easier to estimate than potential benefits which may be of a more intangible nature, for example the benefit of greater staff knowledge which may lead to increased productivity. Because of the significant cost of a simulation analysis it is also important to consider alternative modelling methods which may provide the necessary information. These include such tools as spreadsheet analysis, queuing theory and linear programming. It is important to be aware, however, that although these tools may provide a quicker 'decision', approaches such as queuing theory make a number of assumptions about the system being studied which can provide an inaccurate analysis. The importance of the ability of simulation to model the variability characteristics of a particular system should be carefully considered in these cases. Although simulation can study more complex systems than many analytical techniques, its use may be of limited value for very complex or unpredictable systems. For example, human-based systems, with staff who have discretion in their duties and how they undertake them, present a particular challenge.

Even if a cost-benefit analysis has been made in favour of simulation, a factor that can discount the approach is insufficient time available to complete the project. Activities such as data collection and model building may take longer than is available before a decision is required. The best policy is to consider the use of simulation at an early stage in the decision process. A possible solution is to employ consultants or simulation experts who can reduce the project duration by employing additional staff and can provide a faster model build through the knowledge gained from previous projects.

Simulation and Variability

The use of business analysis techniques such as flow charts and spreadsheets is widespread and well established. However these techniques are unable to capture the range of behaviour of a typical process due to their inability to incorporate dynamic (i.e. time-dependent) behaviour (Profozich, 1998). There are two aspects of dynamic systems which need to be addressed:

Variability

Most business systems contain variability in both the demand on the system (e.g. customer arrivals) and the durations (e.g. customer service times) of activities within the system. The use of fixed (e.g. average) values will provide some indication of performance, but simulation permits the incorporation of statistical distributions and thus provides an indication of both the range and variability of the performance of the system. This is important in customer-based systems when not only is the average performance relevant, but also performance should not drop below a certain level (e.g. customer service time) or customers will be lost. In service systems, two widely used performance measures are an estimate of the maximum queuing time for customers and the utilisation (i.e. percentage time occupied) of the staff serving the customer.

Interdependence

Most systems contain a number of decision points that affect the overall performance of the system. The simulation technique can incorporate statistical distributions to model the likely decision options taken. Also the 'knock-on' effect of many interdependent decisions over time can be assessed using the simulation's ability to show system behaviour over a time period.

To show the effect of variability on systems, a simple example will be presented. A manager of a small shop wishes to predict how long customers wait for service during a typical day. The owner has identified two types of customer, who have different amounts of shopping and so take different amounts of time to serve. Type A customers account for 70 per cent of custom and take on average ten minutes to serve. Type B customers account for 30 per cent of custom and take on average five minutes to serve. The owner has estimated that during an eight hour day, on average the shop will serve 40 customers. The owner then calculates the serve time during a particular day:

Customer A = 0.7 x 40 x 10 minutes = 280 minutes
Customer B = 0.3 x 40 x 5 minutes = 60 minutes
Therefore the total service time = 340 minutes and gives a utilisation of the shop till of 340/480 x 100 = 71%

Thus the owner is confident all customers can be served promptly during a typical day. A simulation model was constructed of this system to estimate the service time for customers. Using a fixed time between customer arrivals of 480/40 = 12 minutes and with a 70 per cent probability of a ten minutes' service time and a 30 per cent probability of a five minutes' service time, the overall service time for customers has a range of between five to ten minutes and no queues are present in this system.

Service Time for Customer (minutes)
Average   8.5
Minimum   5
Maximum   10

However in reality customers will not arrive equally spaced at 12 minute intervals, but will arrive randomly with an average interval of 12 minutes. The simulation is altered to show a time between arrivals following an exponential distribution (the exponential distribution is often used to mimic the behaviour of customer arrivals) with a mean of 12 minutes. The owner was surprised by the simulation results:

Service Time for Customer (minutes)
Average   17
Minimum   5
Maximum   46

The average service time for a customer had doubled to 17 minutes, with a maximum of 46 minutes!

The example demonstrates how the performance of even simple systems can be affected by randomness. Variability would also be present in this system in other areas such as customer service times and the mix of customer types over time. The simulation method is able to incorporate all of these sources of variability to provide a more realistic picture of system performance.

Where is Simulation Used?

Simulation modelling is used in various areas of many different types of organisations. Some examples of simulation use are given below, with reference to industrial case studies published by the author.

Capital Investment

For large capital investments such as equipment and plant, simulation can reduce the risk of implementation at a relatively small cost. Simulation is used to ensure the equipment levels and plant layout is suitable for the planned capacity requirements of the facility (see Greasley, 2000e).

Manufacturing

In order to remain competitive, manufacturing organisations must ensure their systems can meet changing market needs in terms of product mix and capacity levels whilst achieving efficient use of resources. Because of the complex nature of these systems with many interdependent parts, simulation is used extensively to optimise performance. Greasley (1996a) provides a case study of using simulation to optimise a line type manufacturing system by ensuring that each stage in the line has an equal capacity level. Greasley (2000c) provides a case study of the use of simulation to test various scheduling scenarios on a just-in-time production system in order to optimise resource utilisation. Greasley (1999a) provides a case study of the use of simulation to develop production rules that would reduce work-in-progress and production lead-time.

Maintenance

A key customer requirement of any delivered manufactured good or service supplied is its reliability in operation which is often a key measure of service quality. Simulation can test the performance of a system under a number of scenarios both relatively quickly and cheaply. Steps can then be taken in advance to ensure service is maintained under various operating conditions. Greasley (2000a) provides a case study of the use of simulation to ensure that a transportation system can meet demand within a planned maintenance schedule under a variety of scenarios of train breakdown events. Although simulation has traditionally been associated with improving internal efficiency of systems, this is a good example of where it was used not only to prove capability to the maintenance operator, but also to provide a tool to demonstrate to the potential customer that performance targets could be met.

Transportation and Logistics

Transportation systems such as rail and airline services as well as internal systems such as automated guided vehicles (AGVs) can be analysed using simulation. Many simulation software packages have special facilities to model track-based and conveyor type systems and simulation is ideally suited to analyse the complex interactions and knock-on effects that can occur in these systems.

Customer-Service Systems

The productivity of service sector systems has not increased at the rate of manufacturing systems and as the service sector has increased the potential increase in productivity from improving services has been recognised. The use of BPR and other methodologies to streamline service processes has many parallels in techniques used in manufacturing for many years. Simulation is now being used to help analyse many service processes to improve customer service and reduce cost. Greasley (2003a) provides a case study of the use of simulation to analyse a proposed workflow system for a group of estate agency outlets. The purpose of the workflow system is to automate the paper-flow in the house-buying process and thus increase speed of service to the customer. The simulation was used to assist in predicting demand levels on the system, identifying bottlenecks and thus optimise operation before implementation.

BPR Initiatives

Business process re-engineering (BPR) attempts to improve organisational performance by analysis of a business from a process rather than a functional perspective and then redesign these processes to optimise performance. Greasley and Barlow (1998) provide a case study of the use of simulation in the context of a BPR project to redesign the custody operation in a UK police service. Greasley (2000b) and Greasley (2001) present a case study showing how simulation can be used in conjunction with the technique of activity-based-costing (ABC) to show costs from a cost, resource and activity perspective. The cases show how simulation can be used during most stages of a BPR initiative and how the use of simulation can be prioritised and aligned with strategic objectives through the use of techniques such as the balanced scorecard. They also show the ability of simulation to provide a variety of performance measures such as utilisation of people, speed of service delivery and activity cost.

Health Systems

The emphasis on performance measures in government services such as health care has led to the increased use of simulation to analyse systems and provide measures of performance under different configurations.

IT Systems

Simulation is used to predict the performance of the computerisation of processes. This analysis can include both the process performance and the technical performance of the computer network itself, often using specialist network simulation software. An example of using simulation to evaluate the computerisation of a road traffic accident reporting system is provided in Greasley (2003c).

History of Simulation

Simulation has changed both in terms of the software used in implementation and the application areas it is utilised in. Early simulation systems were used in the defence industry in the 1950s and their use in this area is still widespread. These systems used general purpose computer programming languages such as FORTRAN. In the 1960s simulation languages such as GPSS were developed and applications in manufacturing were being developed through the 1970s. The introduction of the personal computer (PC) in the 1980s and the development of sophisticated simulation languages such as SIMAN further increased the popularity of the technique. The introduction of WINDOWS-based systems in the 1990s such as ARENA, WITNESS and SIMFACTORY combined with the business process re-engineering (BPR) movement has widened the application range across the manufacturing and service sector. Simulation systems now incorporate icon-based modelling tools and sophisticated computer animated graphical facilities. Recent developments in simulation include object-based systems and simulation implemented on the World Wide Web.

Future developments are likely to include the greater integration of simulation modelling with computer-based toolkits which support change methodologies such as business process re-engineering. The WINDOWS operating system has permitted greater integration of simulation packages with software such as spreadsheets, databases and draw packages which can be used to share and update data required by the model. Tools such as Visual Basic allow customised menus to be developed at the front-end of systems. Many simulation software packages show their historical roots in an orientation to manufacturing applications. Reflecting the diversity of simulation use, an application-based approach to simulation software is being taken by many simulation software vendors. This allows the simulation software to provide modelling facilities which are focused on a particular application area such as telecommunications or business process re-engineering. Integration with flow charting tools such as VISIO allow the model to be constructed using software already familiar to personnel involved in process redesign. Finally progress will continue in the development of simulation software which is used to control real-time systems such as production control and logistics and thus provide ongoing support for decision-making.

A Classification of Model Types

This section aims to place simulation in the wider context of mathematical modelling methods in order that the correct modelling method can be applied to a problem situation. Models are classed as either static or dynamic, with dynamics systems being modelled using a continuous or discrete-event approach. The techniques of system dynamics and discrete-event simulation to model dynamic systems are described in detail. Figure 1.1 shows the main categories of mathematical models.

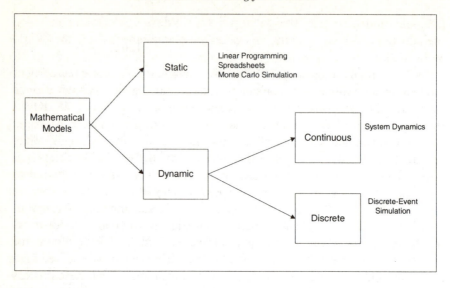

Figure 1.1 Categories of mathematical models

Mathematical models can be classified as either static or dynamic.

Static Models

Static Models include the Linear Programming technique which is an example of an analytical mathematical technique which can be used to solve management decision-making problems. A computer spreadsheet is an example of a numerical static model in which relationships can be constructed and the system behaviour studied for different scenarios. Another example of a static numerical model is the Monte Carlo method. This consists of experimental sampling with random numbers and deriving results based on these. Although random numbers are being used, however, the problems that are being solved are essentially determinate. The Monte Carlo method technique is widely used in risk analysis for assessing the risks and benefits of different, and often very expensive, decisions. Monte Carlo applications are sometimes classified as being simulations, but whereas simulation and Monte Carlo are both numerical computational techniques, simulation applies to dynamic models while Monte Carlo applies to static ones. Software such as CRYSTAL BALL allows the Monte Carlo method to be implemented on a computer spreadsheet.

Dynamic Models

A dynamic mathematical model allows changes in system attributes to be derived as a function of time. The derivation may be made with an analytical solution or with a numerical computation, depending upon the complexity of the model. Models that are of a dynamic nature and cannot be solved analytically must use the simulation approach. A classification is made between continuous and discrete-event simulation model types. A discrete system changes only at discrete points in time. The number of customers in a service system is dependent on individual arrivals and departures of customers over time. The amount of petrol in a tanker being emptied is varying continuously over time and is thus classified as a continuous system. In practice most continuous systems can be modelled as discrete and vice versa at different levels of abstraction. Also systems will usually have a mixture of both discrete and continuous elements. In general continuous models are used at a high level of abstraction, for example investigating cause and effect linkages in organisational systems, whilst discrete models are used to model operational manufacturing and service systems. The system dynamics approach is described as an example of the continuous mathematical model while discrete-event simulation is described under the discrete mathematical modelling approach.

System Dynamics Continuous simulation is used to model systems which vary continually with time. The concept of system dynamics (Forrester, 1961) uses this approach and has become popular as a tool to analyse human-based systems and enable organisational learning (Senge, 1990). System Dynamics attempts to describe human systems in terms of feedback and delays. Negative feedback loops provide a control mechanism which compares the output of a system against a target and adjusts the input to eliminate the difference. Instead of reducing this variance between actual output and target output, positive feedback adds the variance to the output value and thus increases overall variance. Most human systems consist of a number of positive and negative feedback cycles which makes them difficult to understand. Adding to this complexity is the time delay that will occur between the identification of the variation and action taken to eliminate it and the taking of that action and its effect on output. What often occurs is a cycle of overshooting and undershooting the target value until the variance is eliminated. The System Dynamics concept can be implemented using computer software such as STELLA II (Richmond and Peterson, 1994). A system is represented by a number of stocks (also termed levels) and flows (also termed rates). A stock is an accumulation of a resource such as materials and a flow is the movement of this resource that leads to the stock rising, falling or remaining constant. A characteristic of stocks is that they will remain in the system even if flow rates drop to zero and they act to decouple flow rates. An example is a safety stock of finished goods which provides a buffer between a production system which manufacturers them at a constant rate and fluctuating external customer demand for the goods. A system dynamics flow diagram maps out the relationships between stocks and flows. In STELLA II resource flows are represented by a double arrow and information flows by a single arrow. Stocks are represented by rectangles. Converters, which are used for a variety of tasks such as combining flows, are represented by a circle. Figure 1.2 shows a simple system dynamics model in STELLA II format.

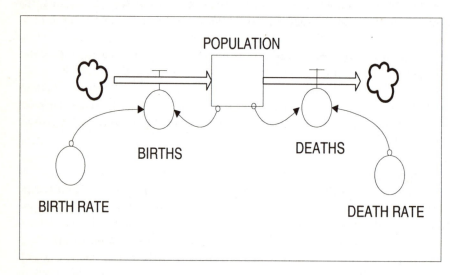

Figure 1.2 System dynamics diagram for population model

Once the diagram is entered it is necessary to enter first order difference equations which compute the changes of a time-slice represented by the time increment *dt*. At the current time point (*t*) the stock value Lev(*t*) is calculated by the software as follows:

$$\text{Lev}(t) = \text{Lev }(t\text{-}dt) + (\text{InRate} - \text{OutRate}) * dt$$

This equation translates to the current stock value is a function of the previously calculated stock value plus the net flow over the time interval since the last calculation. For a population model the following equation could be used to express the POPULATION stock value.

POPULATION (t) = POPULATION $(t\text{-}dt)$ + $(\text{BIRTHS}_{dt}$ - $\text{DEATHS}_{dt})$ * dt

Stahl (1995) demonstrates some of the limitations of the system dynamics approach in an example of a simulation of a new product development process. Here the discrete-event approach is able to model each customer purchase (rather than the quantity sold during a time period) and thus model individual purchase decisions through the ability of discrete-event simulation to carry information regarding each entity (customer) in the system. Also queuing behaviour derived from demand exceeding supply requires the use of the discrete-event method. Rather than as a substitute for the discrete-event method, system dynamics can be seen as a more complementary technique particularly suited to analysing overall cause and effect linkages in human systems. More details on constructing system dynamics models is given in Hannon and Ruth (1994) and Vennix (1996).

Discrete-Event Simulation Discrete-Event simulation is concerned with the modelling of systems that can be represented by a series of events. The simulation describes each discrete event, moving from one to the next as time progresses. This section provides a technical description of how the discrete-event method works. Although simulation software may shield the user from the workings of the discrete-event approach, knowledge of the mechanisms of the method can be particularly useful when verifying model behaviour (Schriber and Brunner, 2000).

When constructing a discrete-event simulation the system being simulated is seen as consisting of a number of entities (e.g. products, people) which have a number of attributes (e.g. product type, age). An entity may consume work in the form of people or a machine, termed a resource. The amount and timing of resource availability may be specified by the model user. Entities may wait in a queue if a resource is not available when required. The main components of a discrete-event simulation are as follows:

- Event - an instantaneous occurrence that may change the state of the system.
- Entity - an object (e.g. component, person) that moves through the simulation, activating events.
- Attribute - a characteristic of an entity. An entity may have several attributes associated with it (e.g. component type).
- Resource - an object (e.g. equipment, person) that provides a service to an entity (e.g. lathe machine, shop assistant).

For a discrete-event simulation a system consists of a number of objects (entity) which flow from point to point in a system while competing with each other for the use of scarce resources (resource). The approach allows many objects to be manipulated at one time by dealing with multiple events at a single point in time on what is called the simulation clock. The attributes of an entity may be used to determine future actions taken by the entities.

In discrete-event simulation time is moved forward in discrete chunks from event to event, ignoring any time between those events. Thus the simulation needs to keep a record of when future events will occur and activate them in time order. These event timings are kept on what is termed the simulation calendar that is a list of all future events in time order. The simulation calendar is also known as the future event list (FEL). The simulation executes by advancing through these events sequentially. When an event has been completed the simulation time - stored as a data value called the simulation clock - is advanced in a discrete step to the time of the next event. This loop behaviour of executing all events at a particular time and then advancing the simulation clock is controlled by the control program or executive of the simulation. There are three main methods of executive control.

In an *event-based* simulation future events are scheduled on an event list. In the first phase of the approach the executive program simply advances the simulation clock to the time of the next event. At the second phase all events at that particular clock time are then executed. Any new events which are derived from these events are added to the simulation calendar. When all events have been executed at the current time the executive program advances the simulation clock to the time of the next event and the loop repeats. The simulation continues until no events remain on the simulation calendar or a termination event is executed.

The *activity-based* approach works by scanning activities at a fixed time interval and activities which satisfy the necessary conditions are immediately scheduled. Unlike the event-based approach, the activity scanning method does not require event lists to be maintained. However the method is relatively inefficient and therefore slow because of the number of unnecessary scans which are needed when no events may be occurring. Also an event may be scheduled between two consecutive scans and thus will not be activated at the correct time.

Most commercial software packages use the *process-based* approach which allows the user to enter a program in a more intuitive flowchart format. The simulation program is built as a series of process flow charts which detail the events through which a class of entity will pass. The use of entity attributes allows decision points to be incorporated into the flow chart, providing alternative process routes for entity classes.

A popular method of control is the *3-phase approach* which combines the event-based and activity-based methods. The three phases are shown in figure 1.3 and described as follows:

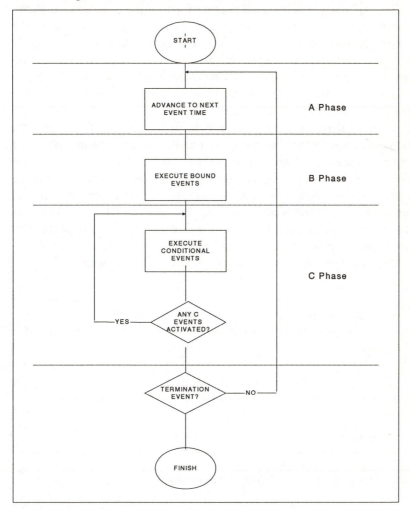

Figure 1.3 The 3-Phase executive

The *'A' Phase* advances the simulation clock to the next event time. The simulation calendar is inspected and the clock jumps directly to the event with the time closest to the current simulation clock time. The clock is held constant during the three phases until the next A phase.

The *'B' Phase* executes all activities whose future time is known (i.e. bound events). The simulation takes all bound events which are due to occur at the current simulation time from the calendar and executes them. The execution of bound events may cause further events to occur. These are placed on the simulation calendar to be activated at the appropriate time.

The *'C' Phase* executes all activities whose future time depends on other events (i.e. conditional events). For each A phase all conditional events are checked to see if the conditions determining whether they can be executed are met. If the conditions are met the conditional event is executed. The execution of a C-event may cause other C-event conditions to be met. For this reason the C-events are repeatedly scanned until all C-event conditions are not met at this time point.

In general bound events are events such as the end of a process when time can be predicted by simply adding the current simulation time to the process duration. Conditional events are occurrences that are dependent on resource availability whose future timing cannot be predicted (e.g. a customer awaiting service at a bank). The 3-phase approach simply scans all conditional events after the bound events have been executed to check if the simulation state allows the conditional event to take place. The operation of the 3-phase discrete-event method can be shown by studying the actions of the next event mechanism on the simulation clock.

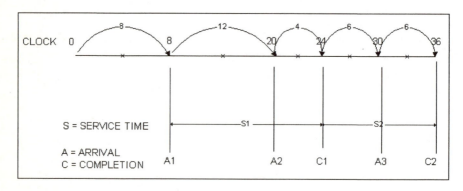

Figure 1.4 Operation of the 3-phase approach

Figure 1.4 illustrates the next-event time advance approach. Arrival times (A1, A2...) and service times (S1, S2...) will normally be random variables taken from a suitable distribution. The discrete-event system operates as follows. The simulation clock advances to the first event at time 8. This is an arrival event (A1) where an entity arrives at the resource. At this time the resource is available ('idle') and so is immediately serviced for 16 time units (S1). During this period the server status is set to 'busy'. The simulation calculates the service completion time (C1) of 24 units and inserts an event on the calendar at that time. At time 20 a second entity arrives (A2). Because the server is currently in the 'busy' state the entity waits at the server queue until the server becomes available. At each future event the status of the server is checked using a conditional (C) event. At time 24 the first entity completes service (C1) and thus changes the server status from 'busy' to 'idle'. Entity 2 will now leave the queue and commence service, changing the server status back from 'idle' to 'busy'. The completion time is calculated as the current time + service time (24+12 = 36) and a completion event is entered on the calendar at this time. At time 30 entity 3 arrives (A3). Again the server is busy so the entity waits at the server queue. At time 36 the second entity completes service (C2) and entity 3 can now leave the queue and commence service. The simulation continues until a termination state is reached. The time in the system for each entity can be calculated by the addition of the queuing time and service time (table 1.1).

Table 1.1 Queue and service times for entities

Entity	Queue Time	Service Time	System Time
1	0	16	16
2	4	12	16

The above demonstrates how the next-event time mechanism increments the simulation clock to the next event on the calendar. At this point the system status is updated and future event times are calculated. The time between each advance will vary depending on the pattern of future events.

Summary

This chapter outlines suitable application areas and reasons for using the simulation modelling method. It is shown that discrete-event simulation is capable of modelling dynamic systems that have the attributes of variability and interdependence. This means that most organisational systems can be modelled using this method and different areas of application within organisations are described. The history of the development of simulation is presented and it is shown that the capability of simulation modelling systems has increased due to advances in computer software and hardware. Finally the techniques of system dynamics and discrete-event simulation are described in more detail.

Exercises

1.1. Past proceedings of the Winter Simulation Conference can be found at www.informs-cs.org/wscpapers.html. Browse the web and find case studies of the use of simulation in various types of organisation. Draw up a table indicating the number of applications by industry sector.

1.2. Categorise each application in question 1.1 by the categories of simulation use outlined in the 'Why Use Simulation?' section.

1.3. Describe how variability and interdependence affect the operation of a railway system.

1.4. Evaluate static, continuous and discrete model types.

1.5. Discuss the advantages and disadvantages of using simulation for problem solving.

1.6. Identify the possible entities, attributes and resources in the following systems:
(a) supermarket
(b) fast-food restaurant
(c) estate agency
(d) bank
(e) car production line.

Chapter 2

Introducing Simulation in the Organisation

Introduction

The use of simulation is both a technical issue involving model development and analysis and a process of the implementation of organisational change. This chapter discusses technical issues such as the selection of simulation software and organisational issues such as the selection of personnel and the acquisition of resources required to provide the capability to undertake a simulation project. It is important that the full costs of introducing simulation are considered, including user time and any necessary training activities. The potential benefits of simulation must also be estimated. One of the reasons simulation is not used more widely is that the benefits from change, undertaken as a result of a simulation study, can be difficult to quantify.

Steps in Introducing Simulation

The steps in introducing simulation in the organisation are outlined:

1. Selection of project sponsor

If the organisation has not utilised the simulation method previously then it may be necessary to assign a person with responsibility for investigating the relevance and feasibility of the approach. This person will ideally have both managerial understanding of the process change that simulation can facilitate and knowledge of data collection and statistical interpretation issues which are required for successful analysis. The development of training schemes for relevant personnel should be investigated so the required mix of skills and experience is present before a project is commenced. It may be necessary to use consultancy experience to guide staff and transfer skills in initial simulation projects.

2. Evaluation of potential benefits of simulation

Often the use of simulation modelling can be justified by the benefits accruing from a single project. However, due to the potentially high set-up costs in terms of the purchase of simulation software and user training needs, the organisation may wish to evaluate the long-term benefits of the technique across a number of potential projects before committing resources to the approach. This assessment would involve the simulation project sponsor and relevant personnel in assessing potential application areas and covering the following points:

- Do potential application areas contain the variability and time-dependent factors which make simulation a suitable analysis tool?
- Do the number and importance of the application areas warrant the investment in the simulation technique?
- Is there existing or potential staff expertise and support to implement the technique?
- Are sufficient funds available for aspects such as software, hardware, training and user time?
- Is suitable simulation software available which will enable the required skills to be obtained by staff within a suitable time frame?
- Will sufficient management support in the relevant business areas be forthcoming in the areas of the supply of data and implementation of changes suggested by the technique?
- Are there opportunities for integration with other process improvement tools such as Process Mapping, Activity Based Costing (ABC) and Workflow Management Systems (WFMS)?
- Does the level of uncertainty/risk in change projects increase the usefulness of simulation as a technique to accept change and increase confidence in implementing new practices?

3. Estimation of resource requirements

The main areas to consider in terms of resource requirements when implementing simulation are as follows:

Software

Most simulation software has an initial cost for the package and an additional cost for an annual maintenance contract which supplies telephone support and upgrades. It is important to ensure that the latest version of the software is utilised as changes in software functionality can substantially enhance the usability of the software and so reduce the amount of user development time required. Most software is available for the WINDOWS platform, but packages are also available for UNIX and other systems.

Hardware

Assuming a dedicated computer is required, costs for a suitable machine should be included. The hardware specification should match the requirements of the simulation software chosen. Maintenance and replacement costs of hardware should be included in cost estimates.

Training

Initial training will speed future software development. Training may be required in both statistical techniques and model development in the software package chosen. Training may be provided by the software supplier, universities or consultancy organisations.

Staff Time

This will be the most expensive aspect of the simulation implementation and can be difficult to predict, especially if simulation personnel are shared with other projects. The developer time required will depend on both the experience of the person in developing simulation models, the complexity of the simulation project and the number of projects it is intended to undertake. Time estimates should also factor in the cost of the time of personnel involved in data collection and other activities in support of the simulation team.

4. Selection of simulation software type

Before the type of discrete-event simulation system is chosen it is important to ensure that the right type of modelling approach is used for the particular problems that may be encountered in the organisation. In general discrete-event simulation modelling can be seen to be appropriate for dynamic systems, i.e. to investigate systems that change over time, but if the decision-maker can recognise the system as a static model, a computer spreadsheet model may be the most appropriate modelling technique to use. Chapter 1 outlines the main types of simulation systems. If it is decided that discrete-event simulation is to be used then before a simulation software package is chosen it is necessary to choose the type of implementation required. The three main categories of simulation systems are as follows:

General Purpose Languages

Computer languages such as FORTRAN, C and C++ have been used for many years to construct simulation models. Davies and O'Keefe (1989) provide computer code for a simulation system using the BASIC and PASCAL computer programming languages. Pidd and Cassel (2000) provide code for a JAVA implementation. Although these languages enable the user maximum flexibility in model building they are now unlikely to be appropriate for business users of the technique due to the greatly increased development times they require compared to a specialised simulation package. A discrete-event spreadsheet simulation system has been developed by the author (Greasley, 1998) using the Visual Basic for Applications (VBA) language which is included with the Microsoft EXCEL spreadsheet. Although not intended for the analysis of complex systems it does enable users to gain 'hands-on' experience of using simulation on the familiar spreadsheet platform. The software also allows the user to see the internal workings of the discrete-event method such as the operation of the event calendar for scheduling future events.

Simulation Languages

Many dedicated simulation programming languages have been developed which hide the workings of the discrete-event system from the user and provide a specialised command language for constructing simulation models. These systems will also provide facilities for tracing the status of the model through time in order to aid model validation. Many systems also incorporate a graphical animated display of the simulation model. Computer languages developed specifically for constructing discrete-event simulation models include SIMAN, SIMSCRIPT, SLAM and GPSS. These provide a much quicker method of building simulation models than using a general purpose language but have the potential disadvantages of the cost of purchasing the software and the time needed to learn the simulation language.

Visual Interactive Modelling (VIM) Systems

Visual interactive modelling systems include ARENA, WITNESS, SIMUL8 and SIMFACTORY. These packages are based on the use of graphic symbols or icons which reduce or eliminate the need to code the simulation model. A model is constructed instead by placing simulation icons on the screen which represent different elements of the model. For example a particular icon could represent a queue. Data is entered into the model by clicking with a mouse on the relevant icon to activate a screen input dialog box. Animation facilities are also incorporated into these packages. For most business applications a VIM system is the most appropriate, although the cost of the software package can be high. VIMs are basically a graphical 'front-end' to a simulation language which takes its information from the parameters of the icons placed on the screen rather than from coding direct. For example the ARENA system is based on the SIMAN simulation language. However these systems do not release the user from the task of understanding the building blocks of the simulation system or understanding statistical issues. Also a complex model may well require recourse to language constructs.

Discussion of Choice of Simulation Software Type

The following discusses the choice available to the user in selecting the most appropriate simulation software package. General purpose software may be applicable when funds are not available to purchase a specialist simulation package or the developer wishes to produce a model which can be distributed amongst a group of people. An example of this is the production of a simulation on a disk for a student cohort. For commercial applications the choice will be between simulation languages and VIMs. The main strength of simulation languages is their relatively low cost and flexibility in the range of models they can produce. They do however have the disadvantage, as with any computer software language, of the need to train users and ensure that programming expertise is not lost when an employee leaves the organisation. Although VIMs usually provide a more restricted range of applications they have the advantage of shorter model build and validation times and are easier to learn. The extra expenditure on VIMs should be recouped through decreased staff costs if the software is used for multiple projects. VIMs are strongly recommended for use by non-technical users or when an end-user approach is taken. However detailed modelling may be difficult within the constraints associated with a VIM. Systems such as ARENA allow the user to incorporate simulation language commands within a VIM model. This increases flexibility, but also brings the disadvantages associated with a simulation language. However whichever simulation software tool is chosen it is likely that for any reasonably complex system some programming will be required (Banks and Gibson, 1997). It must also be noted that using a VIM does not free the user from the need to conduct the statistical aspects of model construction and validation. One approach to package selection is to assess the package according to the needs of a decision support system in terms of the Dialog (interface facilities), Data (database integration) and Modelling (constructs) perspectives (Sprague, 1993).

The dialog component The user dialog must successfully balance the need for ease of use for what may be a casual computer user and flexibility in allowing a number of approaches to solving the problem. The two main dialog approaches are the graphical input system which provides a simple, controlled interface and a command language which provides more flexibility but requires more knowledge of the system. Most decision-makers are unwilling to be trained to use a complex interface and so the command language approach usually requires an intermediary to operate the system. The graphical input system offered by VIM systems is thus usually preferred. Other facilities that help usability include automated input and output analysis help and debugging features and a comprehensive output reporting facility. The visual capabilities of the package should also be taken into account, with features such as automatic animation provided and 3D modelling available. Most VIM systems consist of a draw package which allows a static background to be created using a number of draw and text objects. On this static background a dynamic element is created by defining a moving object shape which moves along a predefined path across the computer screen in response to changes in selected simulation status variables. Performance measures (e.g. queue length, time of customer/product in the system) can also be displayed and are automatically linked to defined simulation variables.

The data component It is important that the simulation package can interface with other software such as spreadsheets and databases which can be used as a store for data used by the simulation. Simulation software has shown developments in this area recently with packages such as ARENA offering connectivity with the Microsoft OFFICE family and the drawing package VISIO through the use of Visual Basic for Applications (VBA). Data should be available for import in a number of textual, logical or graphical formats such as ASCII, spreadsheet, ODBC, DLL and DXF. Numerical data can be used to provide timings for customer arrival or service times for example, and graphical data, such as from a CAD package, can provide the static background graphics. Links to flow charting software such as VISIO can be used to provide both the logical structure of the simulation as well as numerical data information.

The model component   The modelling component itself refers to the language used to construct the simulation model. A range of robust modelling functions is required to create (either from a probability distribution or from a user-defined schedule) and destroy entities (which can represent customers, products, information, etc.) in the model. Functions are also required for modelling decision points which may operate using 'if-then' or probability rules. Resource availability functions should be available which define an availability schedule and overlay on this non-availability due to random occurrences such as machine breakdown events. Functions should be available to assign multiple resources to a particular entity and a particular resource should be assignable to multiple entities in the system. An important aspect of the modelling functionality in a VIM is the ability to extend the standard functions available in the VIM by working at a lower level of programmability. Functionality may be increased further by allowing the user to access system variables and user-defined routines in the source code (usually C or C++) of the simulation software. Functions should also include both discrete and continuous probability distributions for modelling activity and arrival times and resource availability events. Software facilities which provide the 'best-fit' between a range of built-in distributions and user data are also required. Output analysis functions are also required in terms of providing relevant statistical information (e.g. average, standard deviation) over multiple runs of the simulation model.

5. Selection of simulation software package

Once a decision regarding the type of simulation software package (general purpose language, simulation language or visual interactive modelling system) has been made there needs to be a choice of which vendor to supply a particular simulation package. Examples of software in each category are shown in table 2.1.

Table 2.1 Simulation software types

General Purpose language	Simulation language	Visual Interactive Modelling system
PASCAL	SIMAN	ARENA
C	GPSS	WITNESS
Visual Basic	GENETIK	SIMFACTORY
JAVA	SLAM II	PROMODEL

The potential user can read the software tutorial papers from the Winter Simulation Conference available on the internet site www.informs-cs.org/wscpapers.html which provide information of software available. Additional information can be obtained from both vendor representatives (especially a technical specification) and established users on the suitability of software for a particular application area.

Vendors of simulation software can be rated on aspects such as:

- Quality of Vendor (current user base, revenue, length in business)
- Technical Support (type, responsiveness)
- Training (frequency, level, on-site availability)
- Modelling Services (e.g. consultancy experience)
- Cost of Ownership (upgrade policy, run-time licence policy, multi-user policy).

A selection of simulation software supplier details is presented in table 2.2.

Table 2.2 Simulation software vendors

Vendor	Software	Web Address
SIMUL8 Corporation	SIMUL8	www.simul8.com
Micro Analysis and Design	Micro Saint	www.maad.com
ProModel Corporation	ProModel	www.promodel.com
Lanner Inc.	WITNESS	www.lanner.com
Rockwell Software Inc.	ARENA	www.rockwellautomation.com

Simulation software can be bought in a variety of forms including single-user copies and multi-user licences. Most software has a price for the licence and then an additional maintenance charge which covers telephone support and the supply of software upgrades. Some software allows 'run-time' models to be installed on unlicensed machines. This allows use of a completed model, with menu options that allow the selection of scenario parameters. Run-time versions do not allow any changes to the model code or animation display however. It is also possible to obtain student versions (for class use in universities) of software which contain all the features of the full licensed version but are limited in some way such as the size of the model or have disabled save or print functions. The software packages used within this text are ARENA, WITNESS and SIMUL8, three of the most popular simulation packages available (Hlupic, 2000).

6. Identification of computer hardware requirements

Most modern personal computers should be capable of running simulation software. Most software runs on a PC under WINDOWS (although software for other operating systems such as UNIX is available). The PC should have a relatively fast processor (e.g. Pentium) and adequate memory (e.g. 128MB) to allow suitable development and animation speeds. Once the particular package has been selected these details should be easily obtained from the vendor.

7. Identification of training needs

To conduct a simulation modelling project successfully the project team should have skills in the following areas:

General Skills for all Stages of a Simulation Project

- Project Management (ensure project meets time, cost and quality criteria).
- Awareness of the application area. (e.g. knowledge of manufacturing techniques).
- Communication Skills (essential for definition of project objectives and data collection and implementation activities).

Skills Relevant to the Stages of the Simulation Study

- Data Collection (ability to collect detailed and accurate information).
- Process Analysis (ability to map organisational processes).

- Statistical Analysis (input and output data analysis).
- Model Building (simulation software translation).
- Model Validation (ability to critically evaluate model behaviour).
- Implementation (ability to ensure results of study are successfully implemented).

In many organisations it may be required that one person acquires all these skills. Rohrer and Banks (1998) emphasise the need to ensure that care is taken in not only choosing appropriate simulation software but in choosing people to undertake a simulation project that have the required skills. They categorise skills for simulation tasks into *required skills* which must be present before the individual can perform the task, *desired skills* which are optional for performance of the task and *acquired skills* which can be learned as the task is performed. Because of the wide ranging demands that will be made on the simulation analyst it may be necessary to conduct a number of pilot studies in order to identify suitable personnel before training needs are assessed.

Training is required in the steps in conducting a simulation modelling study as presented in this text, as well as training in the particular simulation software that is being used. Most software vendors offer training in their particular software package. If possible it is useful to be able to work through a small case study based on the trainee's organisation in order to maximise the benefit of the training. A separate course of statistical analysis may be also be necessary. Such courses are often run by local university and college establishments. Training courses are also offered by colleges in project management and communication skills. A useful approach is to work with an experienced simulation consultant on early projects in order to ensure that priorities are correctly assigned to the stages of the simulation study. A common mistake is to spend too long on the model building stage before adequate consultation has been made which would achieve a fuller understanding of the problem situation.

The skills needed to successfully undertake a simulation study are varied and it has been found that the main obstacle to performing simulation in-house is not cost or training but the lack of personnel with the required technical background (Cochran et al., 1995). This need for technical skills has meant that most simulation project leaders are systems analysts, in-house simulation developers or external consultants rather than people who are closer to the process such as a shop-floor supervisor. However the need for process owners to be involved in the simulation study can be important in ensuring ongoing use of the technique and that the results of the study are implemented (Greasley, 1996b).

Summary

This chapter has outlined the main steps in providing a capability within the organisation to undertake simulation studies. They are:

- Selection of Project Sponsor
- Evaluation of Potential Benefits of Simulation
- Estimation of Resource Requirements
- Selection of Simulation Software Type
- Selection of Simulation Software Package
- Identification of Computer Hardware Requirements
- Identification of Training Needs.

These steps provide an assessment of the potential costs and benefits of the method and indicate the technical and organisational resources required to implement the technique.

Exercises

2.1. Compare and contrast the three main types of simulation software.

2.2. Search the web at the addresses given for simulation vendors and evaluate their claims for simulation.

2.3. List the stakeholders involved in a simulation project and write a brief description of their roles.

Chapter 3

Formulating a Simulation Project Proposal

Introduction

Simulation modelling is a flexible tool and is capable of analysing most aspects of an organisation. Therefore to ensure the maximum value is gained from using the technique it is necessary to define the areas of the organisation that are key to overall performance and select feasible options for the technique in these areas. This ensures that although simulation may be being used to measure performance at an operational level, the area of usage is based on the strategic needs of the organisation. The first section in this chapter describes the balanced scorecard as a method of linking strategic objectives with operational change.

Another aspect to consider is the nature of the simulation model that is to be developed. In order to assist the decision-making process it is not always necessary to undertake all the stages of a simulation study. For instance the development of the process map may be used to help understanding of a problem. The level of usage of simulation is discussed in this chapter.

There follows a description of project management concepts and an outline of the contents of a simulation project proposal.

Linking Operational Change to Strategic Objectives

In addition to the simulation project plan a business case can be prepared which provides the context for the simulation study by showing how the changes that will be proposed by the study relate to the strategic objectives of the organisation.

One method of linking strategic objectives with operational change is the balanced scorecard (Kaplan and Norton, 1996). A balanced scorecard can be constructed at the organisational or departmental level at which a focused strategy can be adopted. 'A department should have a balanced scorecard if that organisational unit has (or should have) a mission, a strategy, customers (internal or external) and internal processes that enable it to accomplish its mission and strategy' (Kaplan and Norton, 1996). Multiple scorecards can be integrated into a broad corporate framework. The balanced scorecard is more concerned with strategy implementation than formulation. Here it provides a method of identifying business processes for improvement in alignment with strategic objectives.

Strategic objectives are developed across the four perspectives of financial, customer, internal business process and learning. Traditionally financial measures have been used to provide performance objectives, but this approach recognises the fact that financial measures are a measure of past performance and do not directly provide information on how to improve future performance. A cause-effect chain is proposed between financial performance which is dependent on meeting customer needs, which is in turn dependent on the capability of internal business processes, which are in turn dependent on the skills and ability to learn of the organisational staff and systems. The balanced scorecard thus aims to derive objectives for all four perspectives, both external and internal, to improve overall organisational performance. The perspectives are described as below:

- The *financial* perspective is the traditional method used by external agencies in measuring organisational performance. It has the drawback of providing historical information on how the organisation has performed in the past while providing little information on aspects such as the level of performance of business processes that will deliver goods and services in the future. The level of current customer satisfaction is also not taken into account. Thus an exclusive concentration on financial measures may lead to a short-term decision-making approach, with little emphasis on investment directed to long-term excellence in business processes serving customers. A reliance solely on financial indicators also fails to provide a measurement system which takes into account the objectives of multiple stakeholders of a public sector organisation.

- The *customer* perspective assesses the success of the organisation in meeting customer needs. Customer needs can be categorised into factors such as price, quality and speed, on which the product/service wins orders. These factors will also differ between customers and products. By identifying actual customer requirements and deriving measures of success in meeting these (e.g. customer satisfaction ratings) the customer perspective is incorporated.

- The *internal (business process)* perspective focuses on the performance of the organisation's business processes. Objectives for this perspective are typically developed after formulating objectives for the financial and customer perspectives. This perspective provides a link between these external perspectives and the capabilities of the internal business processes of the organisation.

- The *learning and growth* perspective provides the infrastructure in terms of people and systems which enables the organisation to meet the objectives formulated for the financial, customer and internal business process perspectives. This perspective provides a forward looking measure as the ability and success of an organisation in learning new methods or producing new products and processes provides an indication of future performance.

The first step in the balanced scorecard analysis is for the organisation to develop strategic objectives across the four perspectives. Strategic analysis could be approached from a market positioning approach or a core competencies approach.

Market positioning strategy development is when market/customer segments are chosen in which the company will compete and business processes which are critical in meeting these needs are identified. Hill (2000) provides a methodology for linking market needs and operations capabilities for manufacturing organisations. Martilla and James (1977) and Slack and Lewis (2002) provide further models. Once critical business processes have been identified capabilities required for the learning perspective can be derived.

Core competencies strategy development is driven by the exploitation of perceived unique capabilities or resources that the organisation may possess. Here business processes are identified which are required to support the unique capabilities. Capabilities from the learning perspective are derived which support these business processes. Customer/market segments are selected where these capabilities are critical. Whichever method is used a number of objectives with measures and targets should be developed across the four perspectives. For non-profit and government agencies the method can be useful in operationalising improvements when traditional financial measurements provide little guidance on where improvements should be focused. Here the four perspectives allow consideration of stakeholders/customers such as the general public and government as well as staff through the learning perspective.

The Role of Simulation Modelling in Deriving a Balanced Scorecard

The Balanced Scorecard can be viewed as a model itself showing how interdependent elements in the organisation drive future performance. Simulation modelling is usually associated as a tool to assist in business process improvement. However there are potential areas for usage in helping to identify processes for improvement. Firstly the simulation could be used to identify the often complex cause and effect linkages within an organisation between internal business processes and the external customer perspective. The technique could also be used to quantify the amount of leverage business processes have in affecting external measures. This could be achieved by using sensitivity analysis to observe the effect of changes in a business process on external performance. This information could then be used to make decisions regarding the amount of resource and approach adopted by the business process redesign team.

Determining the Level of Usage of the Simulation Model

An important aspect in the process of building a simulation model is to recognise that there are many possible ways of modelling a system. Choices have to be made regarding the level of detail to use in modelling processes and even whether a particular process should be modelled at all. The way to make these choices is to recognise that before the model is built the objectives of the study must be defined clearly. It may even be preferable to build different versions of the model to answer different questions about the system, rather than build a single 'flexible' model that attempts to provide multiple perspectives on a problem. This is because two relatively simple models will be easier to validate and thus there will be a higher level of confidence in their results than a single complex model.

The objective of the simulation technique is to aid decision-making by providing a forum for problem definition and providing information on which decisions can be made. Thus a simulation project does not necessarily require a completed computer model to be a success. At an early stage in the project proposal process the analyst and other interested parties must decide the role of the model building process within the decision-making process itself. Thus in certain circumstances the building of a computer model may not be necessary. However for many complex, interacting systems (i.e. most business systems) the model will be able to provide useful information (not only in the form of performance measures, but indications of cause and effect linkages between variables) which will aid the decision-making process. The focus of the simulation project implementation will be dependent on the intended usage of the model as a decision-making tool (table 3.1).

Table 3.1 Levels of usage of a simulation model

	Level of Usage			
	Problem Definition	**Demo.**	**Scenarios**	**Ongoing Decision Support**
Level of Development	Process Map	Animation	Experimentation	Decision Support System
Level of Interaction	None	None Simple Menu	Menu	Extended Menu
Level of Integration	None	Stand-alone	Stand-alone Database	Stand-Alone Database Real-Time Data

The level of usage categories are defined as follows:

Problem Definition

One of the reasons for using the simulation method is that its approach provides a detailed and systematic way of analysing a problem in order to provide information on which a decision can be made. It is often the case that ambiguities and inconsistencies are apparent in the understanding of a problem during the project proposal formulation stage. It may be that the process of defining the problem may provide the decision-makers with sufficient information on which a decision can be made. In this case model building and quantitative analysis of output from the simulation model may not be required. The outcome from this approach will be a definition of the problem and possibly a process map of the system.

Demonstration

Although the decision-makers may have an understanding of system behaviour, it may be that they wish to demonstrate that understanding to other interested parties. This could be to internal personnel for training purposes or to external personnel to demonstrate capability to perform to an agreed specification. The development of an animated model provides a powerful tool in communicating the behaviour of a complex system over time.

Scenarios

The next level of usage involves the development of a model and experimentation in order to assess system behaviour over a number of scenarios. The model is used to solve a number of pre-defined problems but is not intended for future use. For this reason a simple menu system allowing change of key variables is appropriate. The simulation may use internal data files or limited use of external databases.

Ongoing Decision Support

The most fully developed simulation model must be capable of providing decision support for a number of problems over time. This requires that the model be adapted to provide assistance to new scenarios as they arise. The menu system will need to provide the ability to change a wider range of variables for ongoing use. The level of data integration may require links to company databases to ensure the model is using the latest version of data over time. Links may also be required to real-time data systems to provide ongoing information on process performance. Animation facilities should be developed to assist in understanding cause and effect relationships and the effect of random events such as machine breakdowns.

Integration with shop-floor machine controllers may be necessary for real-time simulation systems. The technical hardware and software capability issues relevant to an integrated system need to be addressed at the project proposal stage to ensure a successful implementation.

If it is envisaged that the client will perform modifications to the simulation model after delivery then the issue of model re-use should be addressed. Re-use issues include ensuring detailed model code documentation is supplied and detailed operating procedures are provided. Training may also be required in model development and statistical methods. Another reason for developing a model with ongoing decision-support capabilities is to increase model confidence and acceptance particularly among non-simulation experts (Muller, 1996).

Managing the Simulation Project

An important aspect of the project management process is identifying and gaining the support of personnel who have an interest in the modelling process. As stated in chapter 2 the developer(s), in addition to the technical skills required to build and analyse the results from a model, must be able

to communicate effectively with people in the client organisation in order
to collect relevant data and communicate model results. The management
of simulation projects has been reported by practitioners as crucial to their
success (Melão and Pidd, 2003). Roles within the project team include the
following:

- *Client* – Sponsor of the simulation project, usually a manager who
  can authorise the time and expenditure required.
- *Model User* – Person who is expected to use the model after
  completion by the modeller. The role of the model user will depend
  on the planned level of usage of the model. A model user will not
  exist for a problem definition exercise, but will require extended
  contact with the developer if the model is to be used for ongoing
  decision-support to ensure all options (e.g. menu option facilities)
  have been incorporated into the design before handover.
- *Data Provider* – Often the main contact for information regarding
  the model may not be directly involved in the modelling outcomes.
  The client must ensure that the data provider feels fully engaged
  with the project and is allocated time for liaison and data collection
  tasks. In addition the modeller must be sensitive to using the data
  provider's time as productively as possible.

The project report should contain the simulation study objectives and a
detailed description of how each stage in the simulation modelling process
will be undertaken. This requires a definition of both the methods to be
used and any resource requirements for the project. It is important to take a
structured approach to the management of the project as there are many
reasons why a project could fail. These include:

- The simulation model does not achieve the objectives stated in the
  project plan through a faulty model design or coding.
- Failure to collect sufficient and relevant data means that the
  simulation results are not valid.
- The system coding or user interface do not permit the flexible use
  of the model to explore scenarios defined in the project plan.
- The information provided by the simulation does not meet the
  needs of the relevant decision-makers.

These diverse problems can derive from a lack of communication leading
to failure to meet business needs, leading to technical failures, such as a
lack of knowledge of statistical issues in experimentation, leading to

invalid model results. For this reason the simulation project manager must have an understanding of both the business and technical issues of the project. The project management process can be classified into the four areas of Estimation, Scheduling/Planning, Monitoring and Control, and Documentation.

Estimation

This entails breaking down the project into the main simulation project stages (data collection, modelling input data, etc.) and allocating resources to each stage such as the time required and skill type of people required along with the requirement for access to resources such as simulation software. These estimates will allow a comparison between project needs and project resources available. If there are insufficient resources available to undertake the project then a decision must be made regarding the nature of the constraints on the project. A Resource Constrained project is limited by resource (i.e. people/software) availability. A Time Constrained project is limited by the project deadline. If the project deadline is immovable then additional resources will need to be requested in the form of additional personnel (internal or external), overtime or additional software licences. If the deadline can be changed then additional resources may not be required as a smaller project team may undertake the project over a longer time period.

Once a feasible plan has been determined a more detailed plan of when activities should occur can be developed. The plan should take into account the difference between effort time (how long someone would normally be expected to take to complete a task) and elapse time which takes into account availability (actual time allocated to project and the number of people undertaking the task) and work rate (skill level) of people involved. In addition a time and cost specification should be presented for the main simulation project stages. A timescale for the presentation of an interim report may also be specified for a larger project. Costings should include the cost of the analyst's time and software/hardware costs. There is then a choice between a 'run-time' license, providing use of the model but not the ability to develop new models, and a 'full' license which is appropriate if the organisation wishes to undertake development work in-house. Although an accurate estimate of the timescale for project completion is required the analyst or simulation client needs to be aware of several factors that may delay the project completion date. The most important factor in the success of a simulation project is to ensure that appropriate members of the organisation are involved in the simulation development. The simulation provides information on which decisions are made within an organisational context, so involvement of interested parties is necessary to ensure confidence and implementation of model results. The need for clear objectives is essential to ensure the correct systems components are modelled at a suitable level of detail. Information must also be supplied for the model build from appropriate personnel to ensure important detail is not missing and false assumptions regarding model behaviour are not made. It is likely that during the simulation process problems with the system design become apparent that require additional modelling and/or analysis. Both analyst and client need to separate between work for the original design and additional activity. The project specification should cover the number of experimental runs that are envisaged for the analysis. Often the client may require additional scenarios tested, which again should be agreed at a required additional time/cost.

Scheduling/Planning

Scheduling involves determining when activities should occur. Steps given in the simulation study are sequential, but in reality they will overlap – the next stage starts before the last one is finished – and are iterative e.g. validate part of the model, go back and collect more data, model build, validate again. This iterative process of building more detail into the model gradually is the recommended approach but can make judging project progress difficult.

Monitoring and Control

A network plan is useful for scheduling overall project progress and ensuring on-time completion but the reality of iterative development may make it difficult to judge actual progress.

Documentation

Interim progress reports are issued to ensure the project is meeting time and cost targets. Documents may also be needed to record any changes to the specification agreed by the project team. Documentation provides traceability. For example data collection sources and content should be available for inspection by users in future in order to ensure validation. Documentation is also needed of all aspects of the model such as coding and the results of the simulation analysis.

The Simulation Project Proposal

The requirements for each section of the simulation project proposal are now given.

Study Objectives

A number of specific study objectives should be derived which will provide a guide to the data needs of the model, set the boundaries of the study (scope), the level of modelling detail and define the experimentation analysis required. It is necessary to refine the study objectives until specific scenarios defined by input variables and measures that can be defined by output variables can be specified. General improvement areas for a project include aspects such as the following:

- Changes in Process Design – Changes to routing, decision points and layout.
- Changes in Resource Availability – Shift patterns, equipment failure.
- Changes in Demand – Forecast pattern of demand on the process.

Many projects will study a combination of the above, but it is important to study each area in turn to establish potential subjects for investigation at the project proposal stage. The next step is to define more specifically the objectives of the study. For example a manufacturing facility may wish to study the effect of machine breakdown on the output of a production line. The objective may be written thus:

> The simulation model will provide a sensitivity analysis of the breakdown rate of machine x on the output units of production line y.

From this the simulation analyst can derive the following requirements from the simulation model specification. Important information on model detail (machine availability), input requirements (breakdown behaviour of machine) and performance measures required (output units of production line) can be implied from the objective stated. The project proposal should contain a number of objectives at such a level of detail which allows the simulation analyst to derive an outline model specification upon which a quotation in terms of time and cost can be prepared. For instance the previous statement requires more clarification on the exact nature of the analysis of breakdowns. For example will an analysis using a simple graph showing breakdown rate versus output suffice? Is it required to show breakdown behaviour under a number of scenarios e.g. additional preventative maintenance measures? These factors may simply require additional simulation runs, or major changes to the model design – so an iterative process of re-defining model objectives between analyst and user is required at this stage.

Once the objectives and experiments have been defined the scope and level of detail can be ascertained. The model scope is the definition of the boundary between what is to be included in the model and what is considered external to the specification. Once the scope has been determined it is necessary to determine the level of detail in which to model elements within the model scope. In order to keep the model complexity low only the minimum model scope and level of detail should be used. Regarding model scope there can be a tendency for the model user to want to include every aspect of a process. However this may entail building such a complex model that the build time and the complexity of interpreting model results may lead to a failed study. Regarding model detail, judgement is required in deciding what elements of the system should be eliminated or simplified to minimise unnecessary detail. An iterative process of model validation and addition of model detail should be followed. Strategies for minimising model detail include:

- Modelling a group of processes by a single process – often the study requires no knowledge of the internal mechanisms within a process and only the process time delay is relevant to overall performance.
- Assuming continuous resource availability – the modelling of shift patterns of personnel or maintenance patterns for machinery may not always be necessary if their effect on performance is small.
- Infrequent events such as personnel absence through sickness or machine breakdown may occur so infrequently that they are not necessary to model.

What is important is that any major assumptions made by the developer at the chosen level of detail are stated explicitly in the simulation report, so that the user is aware of them.

Data Collection and Process Mapping

Once the simulation project objectives have been defined, and the scope and level of detail set, the modeller should prepare a specification of the data required for the model build. It is useful at this stage to identify the source of the information, its form (e.g. documentation, observation, interview) and any personnel responsible for supplying the relevant information. A process map specification should define what processes will be mapped. The process map should provide a medium for obtaining information from a variety of viewpoints regarding the system being organised. In particular, issues of system boundaries (i.e. what to include and what to omit from the analysis) can be addressed (see chapter 4 for more details).

Modelling Input Data

A specification of the type of statistical analysis used for modelling input variables and process durations should be made. A trace driven model will require no statistical analysis of input data, but a forecasting model may require that the data is fitted to a suitable probability distribution. The level of data analysis will depend on the study objectives, time constraints and the amount of raw data available (see chapter 5 for more details).

Building the Model

The simulation software type or the software package used to construct the model should be specified. To allow ongoing use the software should either be available within the organisation or a run-time facility provided (see chapter 6 for more details).

Validation and Verification

Verification or debugging time can be difficult to predict but some estimation of verification time can be made from the estimated complexity and size of the proposed model. Validation will require the analyst to spend time with people who are familiar with the model being studied to ensure model behaviour is appropriate. A number of meetings may be necessary to ensure that the simulation model has sufficient credibility with potential users. Sensitivity analysis may be required to validate a model of a system that does not currently exist. The type of sensitivity analysis envisaged should be defined in the project proposal (see chapter 7 for more details).

Experimentation and Analysis

Experimentation and analysis aims to study the effects which changes in input variables (i.e. scenarios defined in the objectives) have on output variables (i.e. performance measures defined in the objectives) in the model. The number of experiments should be clearly defined as each experiment may take a substantial amount of analysis time. For each experiment the statistical analysis required should be defined. This could include aspects such as statistical tests, use of common random numbers and graphical analysis. The use of a terminating or steady-state analysis should be stated. For example an analysis of breakdown behaviour may require the following experimental analysis:

> The simulation will be run 20 times at five settings of the breakdown rate and the process output noted at each setting. The results will be presented in tabular and graphical format.

See chapter 8 for more details.

Implementation

The results of the simulation study must be presented in report form (chapter 9), which should include full model documentation, study results and recommendations for further studies. An implementation plan may also be specified. The report can be supplemented by a presentation to interested parties. The duration and cost of both of these activities should be estimated. Further allocation of time and money may be required for aspects such as user training, run-time software licence and telephone support from an external consultant (see chapter 9 for more details).

Summary

This chapter provides an indication of how the objectives and performance measures of a simulation study can be derived from the use of a balanced scorecard. It may also be possible to use a simulation model to express the linkages between the four performance measure perspectives of the balanced scorecard. In order to formulate a simulation project proposal the intended usage of the simulation modelling method must be considered. The modelling approach can range from a process map used to clarify current practice to an ongoing decision support system providing day-to-day information. A simulation study should be managed as with any project with the need to provide estimates of time and cost of resources required, scheduling of activities and personnel, monitoring and control to ensure objectives are met within the time and cost constraints and documentation of progress and results. The main elements of a simulation project proposal should indicate the main activities of the project, who will undertake them and a timescale for each project stage.

Exercises

3.1. What benefits and disadvantages does each of the following simulation usages provide?

- Process Map
- Demonstration Simulation
- Stand-Alone Scenario Simulation
- Ongoing Decision Support System.

3.2. Develop a simulation project plan for the analysis of a telephone call centre.

Chapter 4

Data Collection and Process Mapping

Introduction

This chapter introduces the types of data required for a simulation model and possible sources for this information in the organisation. It is anticipated that data collection activities will continue throughout the simulation project lifecycle. Activity cycle diagrams and process maps are introduced as methods of providing a diagrammatic representation of the logic of the process being modelled.

Data Collection

The collection of data is one of the most important and challenging aspects of the simulation modelling process. A model which represents a process will not provide accurate output data unless the input data has been collected and analysed in an appropriate manner. Data requirements for the model can be grouped into two areas. In order to construct the process map which describes the logic of the model (i.e. how the process elements are connected) the process routing and decision points are required as follows:

Logic Data Required for the Process Map

- *Process Routing*　All possible routes of people/components/data through the system.
- *Decision Points*　Decision points can be modelled by conditional (if… then x, else y) or probability (with 0.1, x; with 0.5, y; else z) methods.

In order to undertake the model building stage, further data is required in terms of the process durations, resource availability schedules, demand patterns and the process layout.

Additional Data Required for the Simulation Model

- *Process Timing*　Durations for all relevant processes (e.g. customer service time at a bank – but not the queuing time). Can be a data sample from which a probability distribution is derived.
- *Resource Availability*　Resource availability schedules for all relevant resources, including effects of shift patterns and breakdowns, etc.

- *Demand Pattern* A schedule of demand which 'drives' the model (e.g. customer arrivals).
- *Process Layout* Diagram/schematic of the process which can be used to develop the simulation animation display.

Be sure to distinguish between input data which is what should be collected and output data which is dependent on the input data values. For example customer arrival times would usually be input data while customer queue time is output data, dependent on input values such as customer arrival rate. However, although we would not enter the data collected on queue times into our model we could compare these times to the model results to validate the model.

The required data may not be available in a suitable format, in which case the analyst must either collect the data or find a way of working around the problem. In order to amass the data required it is necessary to use a variety of data sources shown in the table 4.1.

Table 4.1 Sources of data

Data Source	Example
Historical Records	diagrams, schematics, schedules
Observations	time studies, walkthroughs
Interviews	discussion of process steps
Process Owner/Vendor Estimates	process time estimates

Historical records A mass of data may be available within the organisation regarding the system to be modelled in the form of schematic diagrams, production schedules, shift patterns, etc. This data may be in a variety of formats including paper and electronic (e.g. held on a database). However this data may not be in the right format, be incomplete or not relevant for the study in progress. The statistical validity of the data may also be in doubt.

Observations A walkthrough of the process by the analyst is an excellent way of gaining an understanding of the process flow. Time studies can also be used to estimate process parameters when current data is not available.

Interviews An interview with the process owner can assist in the analysis of system behaviour which may not always be documented.

Process owner/vendor estimate Process owner and vendor estimates are used most often when the system to be modelled does not exist and thus no historical data or observation is possible. This approach has the disadvantage of relying on the ability of the process owner (e.g. machine operator, clerk) in remembering past performance. If possible a questionnaire can be used to gather estimates from a number of process owners and the data statistically analysed. Vendor information may also be based on unrealistic assumptions of ideal conditions for equipment operation. If no estimates can be made then the objectives relating to those aspects may need to be changed to remove that aspect of the analysis from the project.

As with other stages of a simulation project data collection is an iterative process with further data collected as the project progresses. For instance statistical tests during the modelling of input data or experimentation phases of development may suggest a need to collect further data in order to improve the accuracy of results. Also the validation process may expose inaccuracies in the model which require further data collection activities. Thus it should be expected that data collection activities will be ongoing throughout the project as the model is refined.

Process Mapping

A process map (also called a conceptual model) should be formulated in line with the scope and level of detail defined within the project specification (chapter 3). An essential component of this activity is to construct a diagrammatic representation of the process in order to provide a basis for understanding between the simulation developer and process owner. Two diagramming methods used in discrete-event simulation are activity cycle diagrams and process maps. Activity cycle diagrams can be used to represent any form of simulation system. Process maps are most suited to representing a process-interaction view that follows the life cycle of an entity (e.g. customer, product) through a system comprising a number of activities with queuing at each process (e.g. waiting for service, equipment). Most simulation applications are of this type and the clear form of the process map makes it the most suitable method in these instances.

Two main problems associated with data are that little useful data is available (when modelling a system that does not yet exist for example) or that the data is not in the correct format. If no data exist you are reliant on estimates from vendors or other parties, rather than samples of actual performance, so this needs to be emphasised during the presentation of any results. An example of data in the wrong format is a customer service time calculated from entering the service queue to completion of service. This data could not be used to approximate the customer service time in the simulation model as you require the service time only. The queuing time will be generated by the model as a consequence of the arrival rate and service time parameters. In this case the client may assume that your data requirements have been met and will specify the time and cost of the simulation project around that. Thus it is important to establish as soon as possible the actual format of the data and its suitability for your needs to avoid misunderstandings later.

A number of factors will impact on how the data collection process is undertaken including the time and cost within which the project must be conducted. Compromises will have to be made on the scale of the data collection activity and so it is important to focus effort on areas where accuracy is important for simulation results and to make clear assumptions made when reporting simulation results. If it has not been possible to collect detailed data in certain areas of the process, it is not sensible to then model in detail that area. Thus there is a close relationship between simulation objectives, model detail and data collection needs. If the impact of the level of data collection on results is not clear, then it is possible to use sensitivity analysis (i.e. trying different data values) to ascertain how much model results are affected by data accuracy. It may be then necessary to either undertake further data collection or quote results over a wide range.

Activity Cycle Diagrams

Activity cycle diagrams can be used to construct a conceptual model of a simulation which uses the event, activity or process orientation. The diagram aims to show the lifecycles of the components in the system. Each component is shown in either of two states, the *dead* state, represented by a circle and the *active* state, represented by a rectangle (figure 4.1). Each component can be shown moving through a number of dead and active states in a sequence that must form a loop. The dead state relates to a conditional ('C') event where the component is waiting for something to happen such as the commencement of a service for example. The active state relates to a bound ('B') event or a service process for example. The duration of the active state is thus known in advance whilst the duration of the dead state cannot be known, because it is dependent on the behaviour of the whole system.

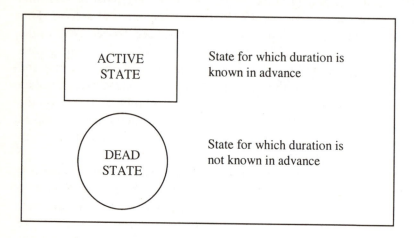

Figure 4.1 Symbols used in activity cycle diagrams

Figure 4.2 provides an example of an activity cycle diagram for a simplified arrest process.

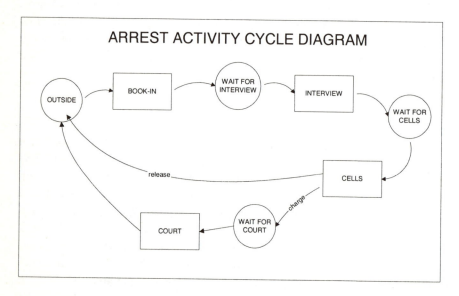

Figure 4.2 Arrest activity cycle diagram

Process Maps

The construction of a process flow diagram is a useful way of understanding and documenting any business process and showing the interrelationships between activities in a process. These diagrams have become widely used in business process re-engineering (BPR) projects and the use of process mapping in this context is evaluated in Peppard and Rowland (1995). Table 4.1 shows the representations used in a simple process flow diagram.

Table 4.1 Symbols used for a process flow diagram

Meaning	Symbol
Process/Activity	▭
Decision Point	◇
Start/End Point	◯
Direction of Flow	→

For larger projects it may be necessary to represent a given process at several levels of detail. Thus a single activity may be shown as a series of sub-activities on a separate diagram. In simulation projects this diagram is often referred to as the simulation conceptual model and the method is particularly suitable when using process oriented simulation languages and Visual Interactive Modelling systems. Figure 4.3 shows a process map for a simplified arrest process.

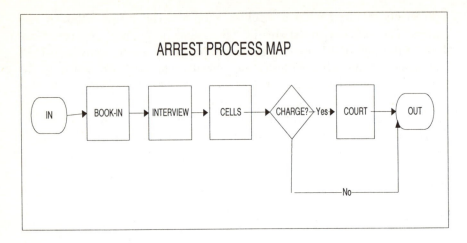

Figure 4.3 Arrest process map

Summary

Once the simulation project proposal has been formulated the next step is to undertake the data collection activities. Logic data consists of the process flow of components within the system and includes the specification of decision points. From this data a process map can be constructed. Further data required includes process timings, resource availability schedules, demand patterns and a schematic of the process layout. Data sources include historical records, observations, interviews and vendor estimates. Two methods of mapping the processes are activity cycle diagrams and process maps. Process maps are well suited to represent the life cycle of an entity (e.g. customer, product) through a system. This method is also widely used in BPR projects.

Exercises

4.1. Draw a process map for an estate agency.

4.2. List the data requirements for a simulation of a supermarket. Suggest a possible data source for each data requirement.

4.3. Sheets of metal enter a machine shop and can go on either of two cutters. The cutter with the smallest queue has preference. The metal can now go through one of three process routes. Lathe, drill and inspect. Drill and inspect. Lathe and inspect. Draw a process map of the process.

Chapter 5

Modelling Input Data

Introduction

It is important to model randomness in such areas as arrival times and process durations. Taking an average value will not give the same behaviour. Queues are often a function of the *variability* of arrival and process times and not simply a consequence of the relationship between arrival interval and process time. The method of modelling randomness used in the simulation will be dependent on the amount of data collected on a particular item. For less then 20 data points a mean value or theoretical distribution must be estimated. Larger samples allow the user to fit the data to a theoretical distribution or to construct an empirical distribution. Theoretical and empirical distributions are classified as either continuous or discrete. Continuous distributions can return any real value quantity and are used to model arrival times and process durations. Discrete distributions return only whole number or integer values and are used to model decision choices or batch sizes. The following table provides guidance on possible methods for modelling randomness.

Table 5.1 Modelling methods by number of data points

Data Points	Suggested Modelling Method
Less than 20	Could use mean, exponential, triangular, normal or uniform
20+	Fit theoretical distribution
200+	Construct empirical distribution
Historical	Trace

Less than 20 Data Points: Estimation

If it is proposed to build a model of a system that has not been built or there is no time for data collection, then an estimate must be made. This can be achieved by questioning interested parties such as the process owner or the equipment vendor for example. A sample size of below 20 is probably too small to fit a theoretical distribution with any statistical confidence although it may be appropriate to construct a histogram to assist in finding a representative distribution.

      The simplest approach is to use a fixed value to represent the data representing an estimate of the mean. Otherwise a theoretical distribution may be chosen based on knowledge and statistical theory. Statistical theory suggests that if the mean value is not very large, interarrival times can be simulated using the exponential distribution. Service times can be simulated using a uniform or symmetric triangular distribution with the minimum and maximum values at a percentage variability from the mean. For example a mean of 100 with a variability of +/- 20% would give values for a triangular distribution of 80 for minimum, 100 for mode and 120 for maximum. The normal distribution may be used when an unbounded (i.e. the lower and upper levels are not specified) shape is required. The normal distribution requires mean and standard deviation parameters. When only the minimum and maximum values are known and behaviour between those values is not known a uniform distribution generates all values with an equal likelihood.

20+ Data Points: Deriving a Theoretical Distribution

For 20+ data points a theoretical distribution can be derived. The standard procedure to match a sample distribution to a theoretical distribution is to construct a histogram of the data and compare the shape of the histogram with a range of theoretical distributions. Once a potential candidate is found it is necessary to estimate the parameters of the distribution which provides the closest fit. The relative 'goodness of fit' can be determined by using an appropriate statistical method. These steps are now outlined:

1. Construct histogram

A histogram is a graphical representation, in the form of a bar graph, of a frequency distribution of a sample of data. A frequency distribution is formed by condensing the data by arranging it into ordered class groupings or categories. The number of class groupings should be dependent on the number of data observations, but a general rule is that there should be at least five class groupings and no more than 15, giving around three to five observations in each class. It is normally desirable to have an equal width for each class grouping. If this is the case the width of each class can be determined using the following equation:

Class Width = Sample Range/Number of class groupings

Thus for a data set with a minimum value of 10 and a maximum value of 58, with 10 class groupings, gives a class width of (58-10)/10 = 4.8, which can be rounded to 5 for convenience.

The next step is to construct a tally chart to count the number of observations in each class interval. The position of a data value within a class interval is now ignored for statistical purposes. Thus all observations within a class (e.g. observations in the range 5 to 10) are now assumed to occur at the midpoint of the range (in this case $(10+5)/2 = 7.5$). It should be noted that with data sets with a relatively small number of observations the choice of class width may alter the distribution pattern formed.

The relative frequency is then calculated for each class by dividing the frequency count in each class by the sample size. A relative frequency histogram can now be plotted for the sample.

2. Compare histogram with theoretical distributions

This stage involves visually comparing the shape of the relative frequency histogram with a range of theoretical distributions. A visual inspection should only be used to provide candidate matches, with a statistical test being used to provide a goodness of fit value which can be compared between different candidates.

The following provides details of some of the potential theoretical distributions that could be used in the matching exercise. Distributions are classified as either continuous or discrete. Continuous distributions are from a range of values, such as a process duration. Discrete distributions are from a number of fixed values, such as a decision point within a model.

Continuous Distributions

Beta The beta distribution is used in project management networks for process duration. It is most often used when there is limited data available from which to derive a distribution. It can also be used to model proportions such as defective items. The parameters shape1 and shape2 provide a wide range of possible distribution shapes.

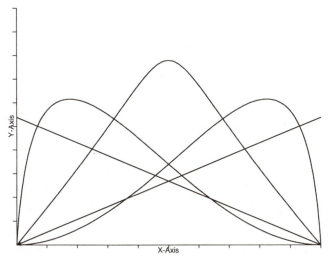

Figure 5.1 Beta (shape1, shape2) distribution

Exponential/Gamma/Erlang The erlang and exponential distributions are a special case of the gamma distribution. The gamma distribution has the parameters shape and scale which determine a wide range of distribution shapes. The distribution is erlang when the shape parameter is an integer and the scale is equal to the mean. The distribution is exponential when the shape has a value of 1 and the scale is equal to the mean. The gamma distribution is used to measure process duration. The erlang distribution is used to model several sequential and independent service phases within one distribution. The parameter k is used to represent the number of service phases. The exponential distribution is used for independent interarrival events or time between process failures.

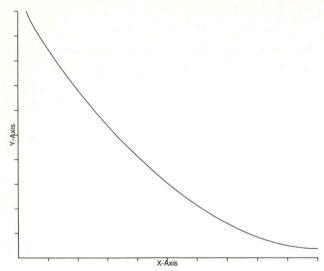

Figure 5.2 Exponential (mean) distribution

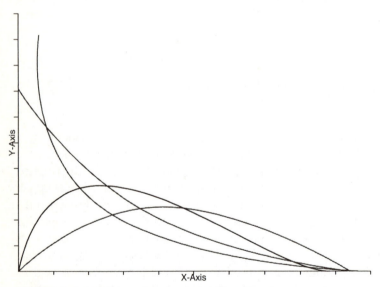

Figure 5.3 Gamma (shape, scale) distribution

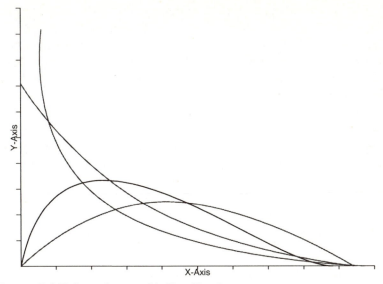

Figure 5.4 Erlang (mean, k) distribution

Lognormal The lognormal distribution is used to model the product of a large number of random quantities. Its shape is similar to the gamma distribution and it can also be used to represent process times.

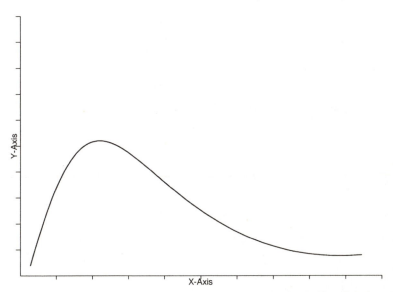

Figure 5.5 Lognormal (mean, standard deviation) distribution

Normal The normal distribution has a symmetrical bell-shaped curve. It is used to represent quantities that are sums of other quantities using the rules of the Central Limit Theorem. This states that when a single process time is the sum of several independent process times, that process time has a distribution which approaches the shape of a normal curve as the number of sub-processes increases. Normality may be assumed however for as little as four sub-processes if the process times for these processes are not heavily skewed. The normal distribution can also be used when a symmetrical distribution is apparent and the mean and standard deviation can be calculated, e.g. dimension measurement for quality inspection purposes.

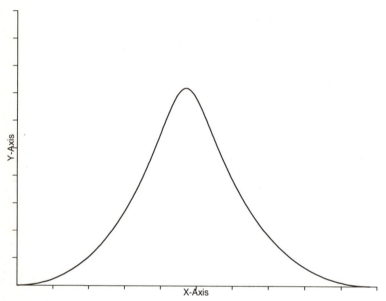

Figure 5.6 Normal (mean, standard deviation) distribution

Triangular   The triangular distribution is difficult to match with any physical process but is useful for an approximate match when few data points are available and the minimum, most likely and maximum values can be estimated.

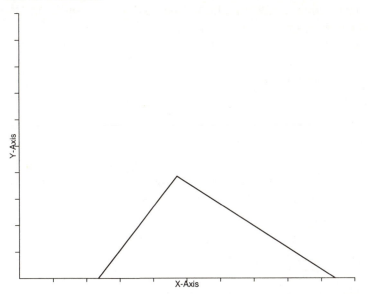

Figure 5.7 Triangular (minimum, mode, maximum) distribution

Uniform This distribution has a rectangular shape and specifies that every value between a minimum and maximum value is equally likely. It is sometimes used when only the range (minimum and maximum) values are known and no further information on the distribution shape is available, but a triangular distribution would usually provide a better alternative. The uniform distribution exists in discrete form also.

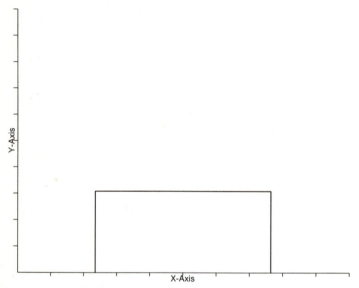

Figure 5.8 Uniform (minimum, maximum) distribution

Weibull The weibull distribution can be used to measure reliability in a system made up of a number of parts. The assumptions are that the parts fail independently and a single part failure will cause a system failure. The distribution can also be used to model process duration.

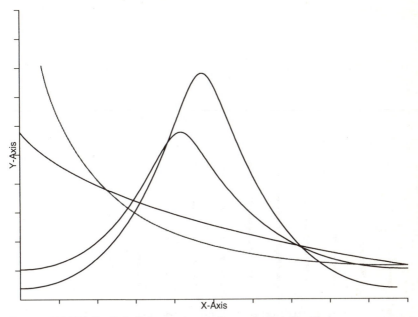

Figure 5.9 Weibull (minimum, maximum) distribution

Discrete Distributions

Binomial The binomial distribution is used to model repeated independent trials such as the number of defective items in a batch or the probability of error.

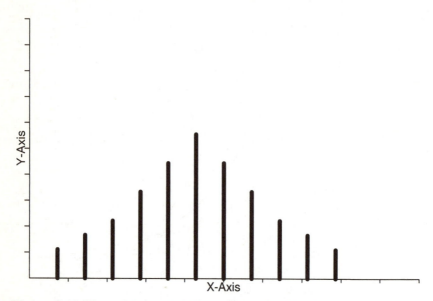

Figure 5.10 Binomial (probability, trials) distribution

Geometric The geometric distribution calculates the number of failures before the first success in a sequence of independent trails. An example is the number of items inspected before encountering the first defect.

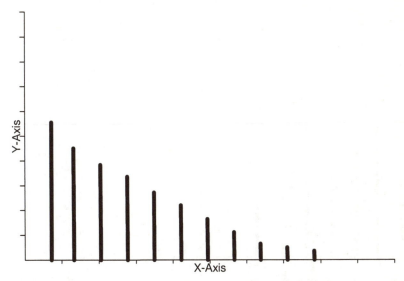

Figure 5.11 Geometric (probability, trials) distribution

Poisson The Poisson distribution can model independent events separated by an interval of time. If the time interval is exponentially distributed, then the number of events that occur in the interval has a Poisson distribution. It can also be used to model random variation in batch sizes.

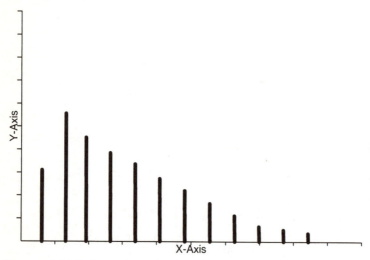

Figure 5.12 Poisson (mean) distribution

Uniform The discrete uniform distribution is used to model an event with several equally likely outcomes and thus generates an integer value between the specified minimum and maximum values. It is used when little is known about the data distribution. The uniform distribution exists in continuous form also.

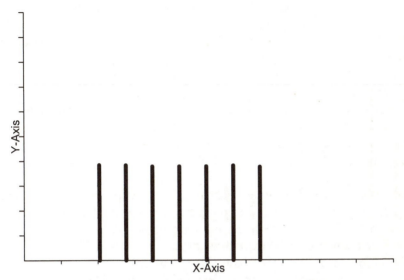

Figure 5.13 Uniform (minimum, maximum) distribution

3. Estimate Parameters

Visual inspection should be used to select a distribution which follows the form of the sample data. The next step is to choose parameters (e.g. mean) for the distribution which provides the closest match to the available data. Note that most simulation input data analysis software will estimate these parameters for you. The following show an approximate method for estimating the distribution parameters. (Law and Kelton (2000) show how parameter estimates for all the above distributions can be found using the more accurate, but more complicated, method of maximum likelihood estimators (MLEs).)

- For the *exponential, lognormal, normal, gamma* and *Poisson* distributions the sample mean and variance (if required) can be calculated to provide an estimate for the parameters.
- For the *erlang* distribution the 'shape' value given for the gamma distribution is rounded to the nearest integer for the 'shape' parameter k. The 'scale' is given by 'shape'/k.
- For the *beta* distribution the parameters shape1 and shape2 can be calculated to provide an estimate for the parameters.
- For the *uniform* distribution the parameters are simply the smallest and largest values in the data set.
- For the *triangular* distribution the minimum and maximum values are simply the smallest and largest values in the data set. The mode can be estimated by multiplying the sample mean by three and subtracting the minimum and maximum values in the data set.
- The *weibull* distribution parameters must be found by forming a maximum likelihood estimator (MLE).

Regardless of which of the above techniques are used the parameters of the theoretical distribution must be estimated from the sample statistics. The most common of these are the mean and standard deviation.

For many applications, such as process durations, it is impossible for the duration to be less than some positive value. This will be represented in the sample data we collect and thus should be represented in the theoretical distribution that we derive from that data. Thus for the distributions earlier discussed that have a range 0 -> infinity (i.e. exponential, gamma, lognormal and Weibull) an additional location parameter is specified which gives the location of the distribution in units to the right of x=0. Law and Kelton (2000) describe the method of maximum product of spacing (MPS) to estimate this parameter which is beyond the scope of this book.

4. Determine the 'Goodness of Fit'

Once a suitable distribution and distribution parameters have been chosen, a visual inspection can be carried out by comparing the shape of a histogram of the data with the distribution. Statistical tests can also be used to determine how good the fit is. The two most popular methods are the chi-square test and the Kolmogorov-Smirnov test. Whatever method or software is chosen to conduct the goodness of fit test, the judgement of the analyst is still required in choosing an appropriate theoretical distribution to describe the sample data. The following issues should be addressed when making a choice of distribution. If a reasonable fit (i.e. high p-value) is not found for any theoretical distribution, check that the sample data is not bimodal (i.e. has more than one peak). If more than one peak is found it may be necessary to define distributions for subsets of the data separately. Otherwise consider using an empirical distribution (see next section) to describe the data. If there is a choice between a number of distributions consider if the data is bounded (minimum and maximum limits fixed) or unbounded (outlying values may occur). Bounded data is more appropriately represented by distributions with minimum and maximum parameters such as the triangular, while unbounded data could be represented by distributions such as the exponential with a parameter of the data sample mean. For sensitivity analysis, distributions with a single mean parameter have the advantage of being easier to adjust than distributions with multiple parameters.

The Chi-Square Test

The chi-square ($\chi 2$) method tests the hypothesis (for an explanation of hypothesis testing see chapter 8) that the data and the chosen distribution fit perfectly and any differences are the result of chance. The following steps can be used:

1. Estimate the distribution parameters from the sample data.
2. State the null hypothesis and decide the significance level to be used.
3. Calculate the expected frequency for each class by multiplying the sample size by the probability specified for the category on the null hypothesis.
4. Calculate the test statistic ($\chi 2$).
5. Calculate the degrees of freedom.
6. Look up critical $\chi 2$ value (by significance level and degrees of freedom) in table and compare the value of $\chi 2$ calculated.
7. If $\chi 2$ calculated is smaller than look up $\chi 2$, do not reject the null hypothesis. If $\chi 2$ calculated is bigger than look up $\chi 2$, reject the null hypothesis.

The $\chi 2$ statistic is calculated as follows:

$$\chi 2 = \Sigma^k (f_o - f_e)^2 / f_e$$
where
k=number of classes
f_o = observed frequency (data) for each class

f_e = expected frequency (distribution) for each class

The degrees of freedom statistic are calculated as follows:

v=k-1-p
where
v=degrees of freedom
k=number of classes
p=number of parameters used in the calculation of the theoretical frequencies, which were estimated from the data sample.

Kolmogorov-Smirnov Test

The Kolmogorov-Smirnov (K-S) test compares the cumulative probability density distributions for the data and theoretical distribution. The K-S test cannot be used for discrete data, thus it is only used for continuous distributions. For discrete data the chi-square test is the only test applicable. For continuous data the K-S test is best for a low sample size when observations within a class fall below the permitted level of five and the degrees of freedom are low. The following steps can be followed:

1. Divide the data and theoretical distributions into classes.
2. Calculate the absolute deviation between the two cumulative distributions for each class.
3. Calculate the K-S statistic as the class deviation with the largest absolute value.
4. Look up (or calculate) K-S statistic and compare with the calculated value.

The following demonstrates goodness of fit tests using EXCEL and ARENA software.

Goodness of Fit Tests using EXCEL

Figure 5.14 shows a chi-square analysis on the EXCEL spreadsheet. The test determines if the data in cells C3:C9 conforms to a Poisson distribution with a mean of 2.4 at a significance level of 0.05. The spreadsheet utilises the EXCEL function POISSON to generate the expected frequency. The frequency of breakdown occurrences is given in column D. The Poisson distribution for the number of breakdowns in column C is given in column E. The formula in cell E3 is =POISSON(C3,C11,FALSE). Column F contains the expected frequency by multiplying the Poisson probability value in column E by the total observed frequency in column D. The formula in cell F3 is E3*D10. The EXCEL CHITEST function is used to test if the observed frequency matches the expected frequency at a level of significance. The formula =CHITEST(D3:D9,F3:F9) in cell F11 provides a p-value () of 0.22603056. In this case this value is greater than the level of significance of 0.05 so the null hypothesis of equal means is accepted (for a more detailed explanation of p-values see chapter 8). Thus we can use a Poisson distribution to represent the breakdown distribution in this case.

	A	B	C	D	E	F	G	
1								
2			breakd(	obs. Freq.	Poisson(x)	expected		
3			0	18	0.09	13.15		
4			1	28	0.22	31.57		
5			2	47	0.26	37.88		
6			3	21	0.21	30.31		
7			4	16	0.13	18.18		
8			5	11	0.06	8.73		
9			6	4	0.02	3.49		
10				145				
11		expected mean	2.4		p-value	0.22603056		
12								
13	p-value of 0.226 is greater than level of significance (0.05) so null hypothesis accepted.							
14	Is a possion distribution at 95% level.							
15								
16	null: the means of both data sets are equal							

Figure 5.14 Chi-square spreadsheet analysis

Figure 5.15 shows a Kolmogorov-Smirnov test on EXCEL. The test determines if the data in cells A2:C9 conforms to an exponential distribution with a mean of 0.1 at a significance level of 0.05. The spreadsheet utilises the EXCEL function EXPONDIST to generate the expected cumulative frequency. The maximum difference between the observed and expected cumulative frequency is compared to a value from a K-S table at a sample size and significance level. Because the calculated value is less then the look up value then we do not reject the null hypothesis of no significant difference, therefore data is exponentially distributed with a mean of 0.1.

Simulation Modelling for Business

	A	B	C	D	E	F	G	H	I	J	K	L
1	data						no.	f	cf	expect cf	difference	
2	1.5	5.5	1.9		0	4	13	0.54	0.54	0.33	0.21	max
3	3.2	4.3	6.5		4	8	5	0.21	0.75	0.55	0.20	
4	4.5	2.1	8.9		8	12	2	0.08	0.83	0.70	0.13	
5	1.4	12.5	2.5		12	16	2	0.08	0.92	0.80	0.12	
6	21.6	14.3	1.7		16	20	0	0.00	0.92	0.86	0.05	
7	1.9	2.4	0.6		20	24	1	0.04	0.96	0.91	0.05	
8	2.3	4.1	3.8		24	28	1	0.04	1.00	0.94	0.06	
9	1.1	9.5	28				24					
10												
11				mean	0.1	K-S table for sample size =24, alpha = 0.05 = 0.27						
12												
13							no./total	cumulate	expondist(number, mean, true)			
14												

Figure 5.15 Kolmogorov-Smirnov spreadsheet analysis

Goodness of Fit Tests using ARENA

The ARENA software incorporates an Input Analyser software utility which provides facilities to derive theoretical distributions. The steps involved in fitting data to either a discrete or continuous theoretical distribution using ARENA are given below.

A sample of one hundred recordings of the 'time between arrivals' in minutes for a customer to a facility has been made and transferred to a spreadsheet. The spreadsheet is saved as a text file with the name 'cust1.dst'. The extension '.dst' is used by ARENA for data files for the Input Analyzer. In ARENA select the Input Analyzer using the Tools/Input Analyzer option. Select File/New and then select File/Data File/Use Existing. Select the file containing the spreadsheet data and a histogram of the data will be generated.

Select the Fit/Fit All option and ARENA will display the nearest fit to the data (measured by the minimum square error) from a range of distribution types. Select Window/Fit All Summary for a ranked (best to worst) list of the fit for all the distributions. This list should be used as a guide only as often a number of distributions will show a similar result on this test and the best-fit distribution should not automatically be chosen. See the 'choosing the distribution' section for guidance. In this case the exponential distribution has been chosen as the most suitable fit. Select the Fit/Exponential option and the results are shown in figure 5.16.

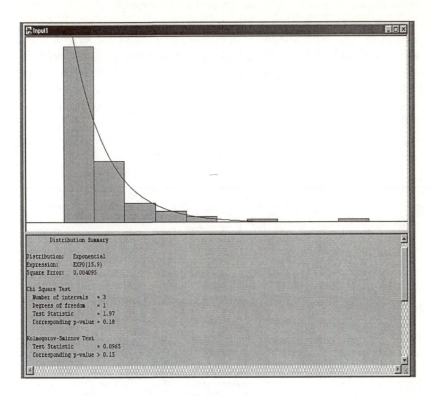

Figure 5.16 ARENA Input Analyzer analysis

Figure 5.16 shows a curve plot of the theoretical distribution superimposed on the sample data histogram. A distribution summary report below the histogram provides information of the specification of the theoretical distribution and the goodness of fit with the sample data. ARENA calculates the parameters for the chosen distribution type. In this case the mean parameter for the exponential distribution is given as 15.9, giving an ARENA expression of EXPO(15.9). The goodness of fit information is given with a chi-square analysis providing a p value of 0.18 and the Kolmogorov-Smirnov analysis providing a p value of greater than 0.15. For these tests a higher p value indicates a better fit between the collected data and the theoretical distribution formed. A p-value of less than around 0.05 indicates a not very good fit while if the p value is greater than 0.1 then we would have a fair degree of confidence that the theoretical distribution represents the data, assuming that the sample size is sufficient for the test. For a more detailed explanation of p-values see chapter 8.

200+ Data Points: Constructing an Empirical Distribution

For more than 200 data points the option of constructing a user-defined distribution is available. An empirical or user-defined distribution is a distribution that has been obtained directly from the sample data. An empirical distribution is usually chosen if a reasonable fit cannot be made with the data and a theoretical distribution. It is usually necessary to have in excess of 200 data points to form an empirical distribution. In order to convert the sample data into an empirical distribution the data is converted into a cumulative probability distribution using the following steps:

1. Sort values into ascending order.
2. Group identical values (discrete) or group into classes (continuous).
3. Compute the relative frequency of each class.
4. Compute the cumulative probability distribution of each class.

Constructing an Empirical Distribution Example

Data has been collected on interarrival times. The data has been sorted into the following classes of width 20 time units.

Table 5.2 Interarrival time frequency distribution

Interarrival Time (Class)	Frequency	Relative Frequency	Cumulative Frequency
0 to under 20	58	0.48	0.48
20 to under 40	44	0.37	0.85
40 to under 60	13	0.11	0.96
60 to under 80	5	0.04	1.00

It can be shown that for a continuous empirical distribution the value of a random value, X (in this case the interarrival time) is given by:

$$X = (R - r_i)/a_i + x_i$$

where
R = random number between 0 and 1
i = class containing random number
x_i = value of X at the ith class
r_i = cumulative probability at the ith class

a_i =gradient of the relative class = $(r_{i+1} - r_i)/(x_{i+1} - x_i)$
where
x_{i+1} = value of X at the $_{i+1}$th class
r_{i+1} = cumulative probability at the $_{i+1}$th class

Thus for a generated random number of 0.35, the interarrival time (X) would be calculated as follows:-
i=1
$a_i = (0.48 - 0)/(20 - 0) = 0.024$
$X = (0.35 - 0)/0.024 + 0 = 14.58$

Note that the method takes into account the shape of the distribution within the classes and does not simply take the midpoint value. (Thus all random numbers generated between 0 and 0.48 would not give an interarrival time of 10.) In a simulation model the simulation software would generate a random number between 0 and 1 and the interarrival time would be interpolated using the above equations.

Constructing an Empirical Distribution with ARENA

The ARENA Input Analyzer allows both discrete and continuous empirical distributions to be formed using the Fit/Empirical option. In ARENA select the Input Analyzer using the Tools/Input Analyzer option. Select File/New and then select File/Data File/Use Existing. Select the file containing the data and a histogram of the data will be generated. Select the Fit/Empirical option and ARENA will display the empirical distribution as in figure 5.17.

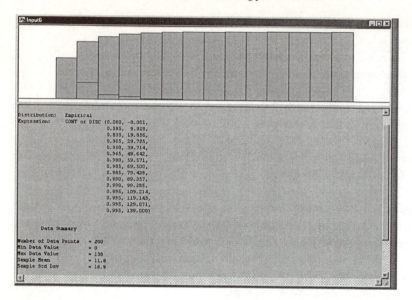

Figure 5.17 ARENA Input analyzer empirical distribution

The distribution is given a list of probabilities and values to return a real valued quantity. The values given by the Input Analyzer should be used in conjunction with the ARENA CONTINUOUS expression. The values are interpreted as follows. 0.595, 9.928 provides a 59.5% chance that the number generated will be between 0 and 9.928. 0.835, 19.856 provides a 24% (0.835 – 0.595) chance that the number generated will be between 9.928 and 19.856 and so on.

Constructing an Empirical Distribution with SIMUL8

Select Trials/Distributions/New/Probability Profile Distribution. Give your distribution a name. Choose between a discrete or continuous empirical distribution. Click on the bars in the graphical display and enter the relative frequency of each bar as a percentage. Right click for options to add and delete bars. The named distribution can now be used in your model (see figure 5.18).

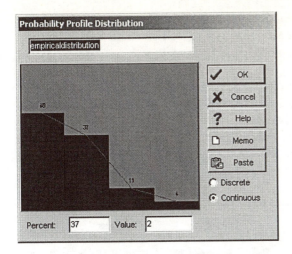

Figure 5.18 Constructing an empirical distribution using SIMUL8

Historical Data Points

A simulation driven by historical data is termed a 'trace-driven' simulation. An example would be using actual arrival times of customers in a bank directly in the simulation model. The major drawback of this approach is that it prevents the simulation from being used in the 'what-if' mode as only the historical data is modelled. It also does not take account of the fact that in the future the system will most likely encounter conditions out of the range of the sample data used. This approach can be useful however in validating model performance when the behaviour of the model can be compared to the real system with identical data.

Nonstationary Arrival Processes

Arrivals in many systems are modelled as stationary Poisson processes in which arrivals occur one at a time, are independent and the average rate is constant over time. This is equivalent to an interarrival time with an exponential distribution and a fixed mean. However many arrival patterns such as customer arrivals in service systems vary greatly with time due to outside factors such as lunch breaks and customer behaviour and are thus modelled as nonstationary Poisson processes. In order to model this behaviour, periods of time when the arrival rate remains constant must be identified and an arrival rate calculated for each time period per unit of time. It should be noted that simply changing the parameter (e.g. mean) value of the distribution for each time period will generally cause incorrect results and the following method should be used:

1. Determine the maximum arrival rate for all time periods.
2. Generate arrivals using a stationary Poisson process (i.e. exponential distribution between arrivals).
3. 'Thin-out' the arrivals by only allowing them to enter the system with a probability of the arrival rate for the current time period divided by the maximum arrival rate determined in step 1.

Summary

This chapter has covered the following methods for modelling input data in a simulation model:

1. Estimation.
2. Deriving a theoretical distribution.
3. Constructing an empirical distribution.
4. Using historical data.

Ideally a sample of measures should be available from which variability can be modelled. From a sample of the required size the two approaches are to either 'fit' (i.e. find the closest match) a theoretical distribution to the sample or to construct a user-defined (empirical) distribution from the sample. The choice of approach to take will depend on the circumstances of the project but it is recommended that a theoretical distribution be used for sample sizes over 20. An empirical distribution can also be used for sample sizes over 200 (Banks and Gibson, 1998).

Table 5.2 provides guidance on modelling input data:

Table 5.2 Modelling input data methods

	Disadvantages	Advantages	Comments
Estimation	Lack of accuracy.	Only option.	
Fit Theoretical Distribution	No available theoretical distributions may fit data. Generates values outside of the data range which may not be appropriate.	Can 'smooth' data to the underlying distribution. Generates values outside of data sampled. Compact method of representing data values. Distribution easy to scale for sensitivity analysis.	Best choice if a reasonable data fit can be made.
Construct Empirical Distribution	'Irregular' distribution may be formed if data sample is not large. Cannot usually generate values outside of range of data (therefore may miss 'extreme' values). Difficult to scale for sensitivity analysis. Can be cumbersome to incorporate large data set in simulation.	Provides distribution when no theoretical distribution provides an adequate fit to data.	Use if no theoretical distribution can be fit.
Historical Data	Only reproduces historical behaviour.	Can assist in model validation.	Use as a validation tool.

Exercises

5.1. Compare the process of deriving a theoretical and empirical distribution.

5.2. A number of observations have been made of arrivals to a supermarket. The frequency of arrivals in a ten minute period are as follows.

Number of Arrivals	Frequency
0	70
1	80
2	34
3	12
4	4
Total	200

Using a chi-square goodness of fit test, find if the arrivals can be described by a Poisson distribution with a mean of 1 at a significance level of 0.1.

5.3. A number of observations have been taken of customers being served at a cafeteria. Analysis has revealed a mean of two minutes and a standard deviation of 0.5 minutes for the data. Investigate using a Kolmogorov-Smirnov test that the observations are normally distributed at a significance level of 0.1.

Serve Time (minutes)	Observed Relative Cumulative Frequency
Less than 1	0.02
Less than 2	0.29
Less than 3	0.54
Less than 4	0.59
Less than 5	0.90
Less than 6	0.95
Less than 7	1.00

5.4. The following data has been collected of arrival times.

4.9	4.4	3.8	5.9	4.6
2.9	3.9	3.8	6.8	5.3
3.5	1.3	3.1	4.3	3.5
6.5	5.3	4.6	5.1	3.5
5.4	4.3	4.7	3.7	3.8
5.5	2.6	6.2	4.5	8.8
3.3	6.5	7.2	2.8	6.2
5.0	6.9	3.9	7.6	5.3
2.7	1.9	2.0	5.2	4.6
5.1	4.3	2.4	4.6	7.9

Find the parameters of an empirical distribution that fits the data above.

Chapter 6

Building the Model

Introduction

This chapter describes the model building process which involves using computer software to translate the process map into a computer simulation model which can be 'run' to generate model results. The use of the VIM systems ARENA, WITNESS and SIMUL8 will be demonstrated using a simple case study of a bank clerk system. As stated in chapter 2, these packages have been chosen as they represent three of the most popular VIM systems in use. Note that the models built in this chapter incorporate probability distributions and so the results may differ slightly to those in the text, due to random variation. The results from the same model run on different simulation software may also vary.

The Single Queue Bank Clerk Simulation

A bank clerk services two types of customer. The time between customer arrivals is exponentially distributed with a mean of 15 minutes for customer type 1 and 10 minutes for customer type 2. The processing time for type 1 customers is uniformly distributed between two and six minutes and between four and ten minutes for type 2 customers. Performance statistics are required on the average time a customer is in the system which includes both queue time and service time. Two versions of the bank clerk systems will be simulated. A single queue system where both types of customers form a queue at a service till staffed by two members of staff. An alternative dual queue system is then modelled. This incorporates a decision rule that directs customers to one of two service tills depending on which till queue holds the minimum number of customers. In chapter 8 statistical techniques are used to determine if there is a statistically significant difference between the performance of the two systems. The process map for the single queue bank clerk simulation is shown in figure 6.1. The two types of customer arrive from outside the system and are processed by one of two bank clerks. They then leave the system after the process has been completed.

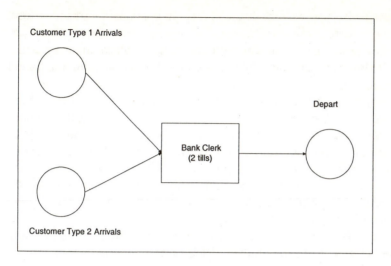

Figure 6.1 Process map of single queue bank clerk simulation

Building the Model using ARENA

When the ARENA system is run the screen display in figure 6.2 should be displayed.

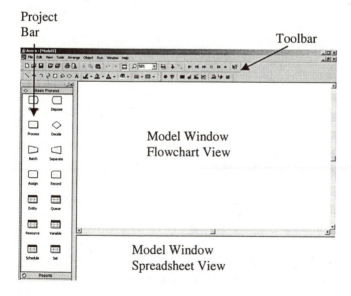

Figure 6.2 ARENA BASIC model window

The project bar to the left of the screen display contains the modules from which you construct the simulation by dragging them on to the model window flowchart view. Data can be entered into each module by either double clicking each module to obtain a dialog box or by using the model window spreadsheet view.

Figure 6.3 shows the modules required for the single queue bank clerk simulation placed on the flowchart view screen. Two create modules are used to generate the two types of bank customers. Two assign modules are used to set the process time for each customer type. A process module is used to represent the bank clerk resource. A dispose module is used to simulate the customers leaving the bank. The modules will automatically connect together to define the relationship between the modules if they are entered on the screen in order from left to right. If the modules are not connected by the connecting lines they can be connected manually using the connect button ▣ on the toolbar. Click on the connect button and the cursor will change to a cross hair. Then click on the exit point (▶) of the first module and click on the entry point (■) of the module you wish to connect to. The connection will then be made. To remove a connection, click on the connection line to highlight it and press the Del key on your keyboard.

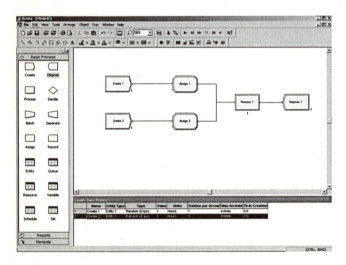

Figure 6.3 Enter the modules on the flowchart view screen

Double click on the create 1 module and the dialog box will appear as in figure 6.4. For the name parameter enter customer type 1 arrivals. For the type parameter select Random (Expo) and for the value parameter enter 15.

The module will then create customer arrivals which are exponentially distributed with a mean of 15 minutes. Repeat the same for the create 2 module but give this the name parameter customer type 2 arrivals and enter a value parameter of 10 to give a customer arrival rate with an exponential distribution with a mean of ten minutes.

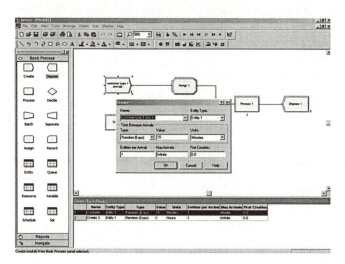

Figure 6.4 Enter the create module parameters

Double click on the assign 1 module and the dialog box will appear as in figure 6.5. Click on the add button and select attribute for type. Type in processtime for attribute name and UNIFORM(2,6) for the new value. This sets the attribute (value which is carried with the entity/customer through the simulation) called processtime to a uniform distribution with a lower bound of two minutes and a upper bound of six minutes. Repeat the same for the assign 2 module but set the processtime attribute to UNIFORM(4,10).

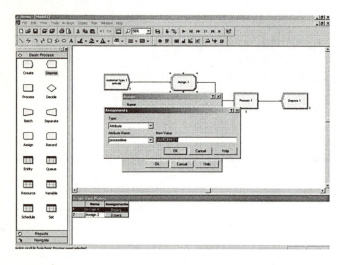

Figure 6.5 Assign the processtime attribute

The process module can be used to represent a resource such as a machine or person. In this case it is representing the bank clerk. Double click on the process module to observe the dialog box as in figure 6.6. Set the seize/delay/release option from the action menu. Click on the add button and enter bank clerk for the resource name. Select the constant option for the delay type. Select the units as minutes and enter processtime for the value parameter. This sets the process duration as the value assigned to this attribute for each customer type in the previous assign module.

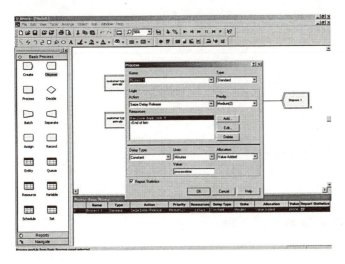

Figure 6.6 Entering the process module parameters

Click on the resource module in the project bar. A spreadsheet view of the currently defined resources should appear in the model window spreadsheet view (figure 6.7). A bank clerk resource was automatically created when this was entered in the process module. Change the capacity entry from 1 to 2 to fix a maximum capacity level of two bank clerks.

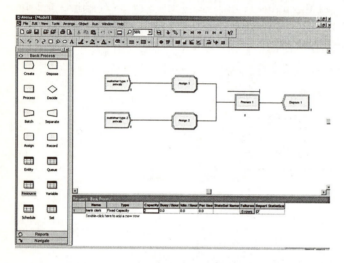

Figure 6.7 Setting the bank clerk capacity

Select the Run/Setup/Replication Parameters option from the menu bar. The dialog box shown in figure 6.8 should appear. Set the replication length to 480 and all unit entries as minutes.

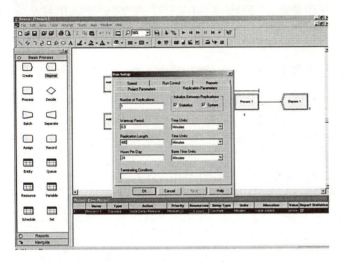

Figure 6.8 Setting the simulation run length

A variety of reports are available in ARENA. In order to provide information on the customer time in system select the Run/Setup/Reports option (figure 6.9). Select the default report as SIMAN Summary Report (.out file).

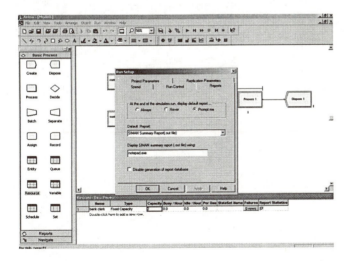

Figure 6.9 Setting the output report format

Run the model by clicking on the run icon (▶) on the toolbar. The simulation can be stopped at any time using the stop icon (■). When the simulation has completed its run the output report (figure 6.10) will appear. In this case the average time in system for the customer is given as 6.29 minutes with a minimum time of 2.01 minutes and a maximum time of 11.02 minutes.

```
                       ARENA Simulation Results
                 Aston Business School - License: 2500000142

                      Summary for Replication 1 of 1

Project:unnamed Project                    Run execution date :12/19/2002
Analyst:Aston Business School              Model revision date:12/19/2002

Replication ended at time      : 480.0

                            TALLY VARIABLES

Identifier            Average   Half width  Minimum    Maximum   Observations

Entity 1.VATime       5.7178    (Insuf)     2.0123     9.9383       68
Entity 1.NVATime       .00000   (Insuf)      .00000     .00000      68
Entity 1.WaitTime      .52867   (Insuf)      .00000    5.5848       68
Entity 1.TranTime      .00000   (Insuf)      .00000     .00000      68
Entity 1.OtherTime     .00000   (Insuf)      .00000     .00000      68
Entity 1.TotalTime    6.2864    (Insuf)     2.0123    11.021        68
Process 1.Queue.Waitin .52100   (Insuf)      .00000    5.5848       69

                       DISCRETE-CHANGE VARIABLES

Identifier            Average   Half width  Minimum    Maximum   Final value

tis                   5.9685    (Insuf)      .00000    11.021     9.6138
Entity 1.WIP           .91032   (Insuf)      .00000    4.0000     1.0000
bank clerk.NumberBusy  .83343   (Insuf)      .00000    2.0000     1.0000
bank clerk.NumberSched 2.0000   (Insuf)     2.0000     2.0000     2.0000
bank clerk.Utilization .41771   (Insuf)      .00000    1.0000      .50000
Process 1.Queue.Number .07489   (Insuf)      .00000    2.0000      .00000

                             OUTPUTS

             Identifier                  Value

             single queue time in sy     6.2864
             Entity 1.NumberIn          69.000
             Entity 1.NumberOut         68.000
             bank clerk.TimesUsed       69.000
             bank clerk.ScheduledUti     .41771
             System.NumberOut           68.000

Simulation run time: 0.02 minutes.
Simulation run complete.
```

Figure 6.10 ARENA simulation report

Building the Model using SIMUL8

To build a simulation using the SIMUL8 software you enter a number of objects on the screen such as work centres and queues. Routing arrows define the route that work items take as they move through the simulation. When the SIMUL8 software is run the screen is shown as in figure 6.11.

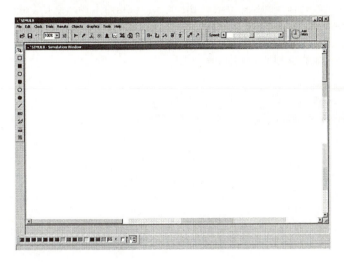

Figure 6.11 SIMUL8 screen display

To build the model, place two work entry points on the screen by clicking on the work entry point icon (🖳) and then clicking again on the screen. The work entry points are used to create new entities in the model. There must be two work entry points for the single queue to prevent the two bank clerk resources 'doubling up' when one customer is being served. Add the storage area using the storage area icon (🖳). This acts as a queuing area for entities. Add the two work centres using the work centre icon (🖳). This represents a resource such as equipment or staff. Finally a work exit point is added using the work exit point icon (🖳). This acts as an exit point for the entities. The screen should be as figure 6.12.

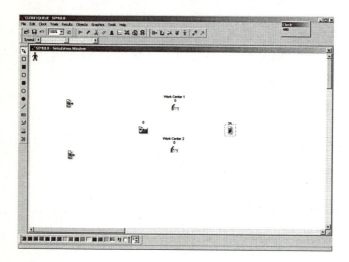

Figure 6.12 Adding bank clerk elements

The next stage is to add information to the model objects that have been placed on the screen. First set the interarrival times for entities at the work entry points. Double click on work entry point 1 and set the distribution element to exponential using the pull-down list. Enter 15 for the average value (figure 6.13). For work entry point 2 set the distribution element to exponential and the parameter to 10.

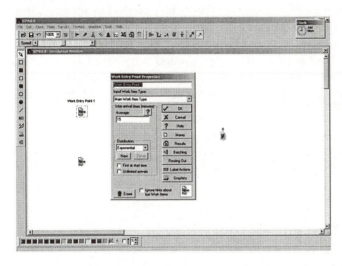

Figure 6.13 Setting the work entry point interarrival times

Because both customer types now flow to both work centres it is necessary to set a process time for each customer type on entry to the system at the work entry points rather than at the work centres. This is achieved by setting an entity attribute named processtime and using this attribute to set the processing time at the work centre. Double click on the work entry point 1 icon and then click on the label actions button. Click on the add button, click on new and enter the name processtime to define the attribute. Click on the OK buttons to return to the work entry properties screen. Click on the label actions button, click on the set to option, then select the value option. Select the distribution as uniform from the pull-down menu and enter a lower bound value of 2 and a upper bound entry of 6 (figure 6.14). Repeat this procedure (there is no need to define the processtime attribute again) for the work entry point 2 with parameters of 4 and 10 for the uniform distribution.

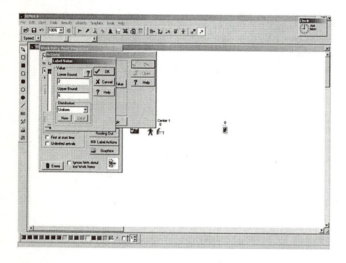

Figure 6.14 Setting the work centre process time

It is now necessary to ensure that the processtime attribute which has been set at the work entry points is used for the process duration at the work centre. To do this double click on work centre 1 and select the distribution as fixed. Enter the name processtime for the fixed value (figure 6.15). Repeat the process for work centre 2.

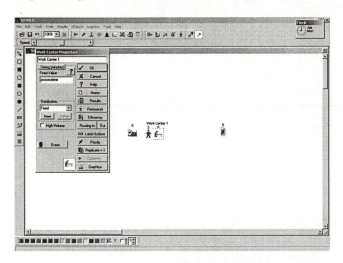

Figure 6.15 Setting the work centre process duration

Simulation Modelling for Business

The next step is to create the resource which will be utilised at the work centre. Double click on work centre 1 and click on the resources button. Click on Add, then New to create a new resource. Specify the capacity as 1. Enter the name bank clerk (figure 6.16). Repeat this for work centre 2.

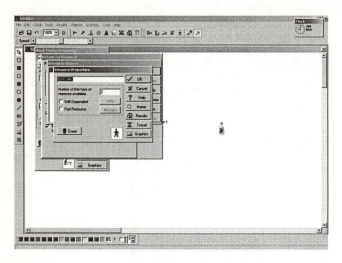

Figure 6.16 Defining the bank clerk resource

The final step before we can run the model is to connect the screen objects to define the default routes for entity flow. The route lines can be seen at any time by clicking on the Show/Hide route arrows button (⌧). To define new route lines click on the route drawing mode button (⌧) on the toolbar. Click on work entry point 1 and move to storage area 1 and click again. A line showing the route defined should appear on the screen. Repeat this process to connect work entry point 2 to storage area 1. Then connect the storage area 1 to the work centre 1 and work centre 2 objects. Finally link work centre 1 to work complete 1 (figure 6.17). Route lines can be deleted by repeating the process for a route line that already exists (i.e. clicking on its from and to points in route drawing mode).

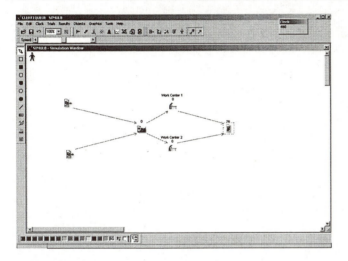

Figure 6.17 Defining the simulation routes

In order to set the time in minutes for the simulation to run select the Trials menu option on the toolbar and enter 480 minutes for the results collection period. Run the simulation by clicking on the run button (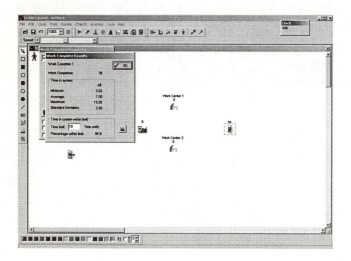) on the toolbar. When the simulation has completed its run, double click on the work complete 1 icon and click on the results button. Summary results are presented for the time in system for customers in the bank clerk system (figure 6.18). In this case the average time in the system for a customer is given as 7.00 minutes, with a minimum time of 2.02 minutes and a maximum time of 13.35 minutes.

Figure 6.18 Bank clerk summary results screen

Building the Model using WITNESS

Open the model startup.mod, which is located in the demo/tutorial subdirectory of your WITNESS installation and the screen display in figure 6.19 should be shown. Elements are added to the WITNESS simulation by clicking on the required element in the designer element window and then clicking again at the required location in the simulation window. Elements can be moved in the simulation window by clicking on them and holding down the left mouse button to allow them to be dragged around the screen area. To enter data for each element in the simulation window double click on the element to obtain a detail dialog box.

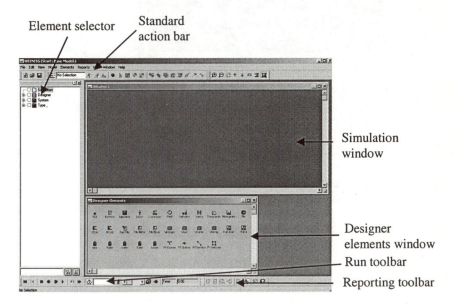

Figure 6.19 WITNESS model window

Figure 6.20 shows the elements required for the single queue bank clerk simulation. Place two part elements on the screen by clicking on the part element in the designer elements window and clicking again in the simulation window. Repeat the process for the queue and machine elements. Finally add a real number attribute element by clicking on the Rattr element and clicking again in the simulation window.

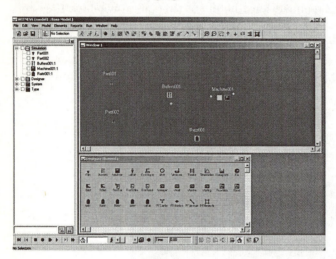

Figure 6.20 Adding the bank clerk elements

The next stage is to add information to the simulation elements that have been placed in the simulation window. Because both customer types now flow to both machines (clerks) it is necessary to set a process time for each customer type on entry to the system rather than at the machines (clerks). This is achieved by setting an entity attribute named processtime and using this attribute to set the processing time at the work centre. Double click on the Rattr attribute element and enter the name processtime (figure 6.21).

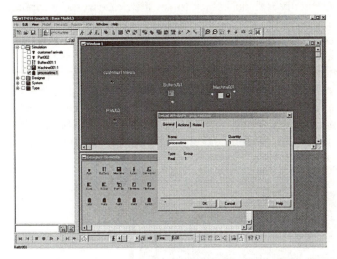

Figure 6.21 Entering the attribute detail information

The next step is to define the part detail information. Double click on the part001 element. Enter the name customer1arrivals. Choose type as active and enter Gamma(1,15,1) as the first arrival time and interarrival time. There is no separate exponential distribution in WITNESS but a gamma distribution with an alpha value (shape) of 1 and a beta value (scale) equal to the mean is equivalent. The term Gamma(1,15,1) gives a gamma distribution with an alpha value of 1, a mean of 15 minutes and a random number stream of 1. Finally it is necessary to set the processtime attribute for customer type 1 arrivals. Click on the 'Actions on Create' button and enter the term processtime=UNIFORM(2,6,1) to set the process time for customer type 1 at a uniform distribution with a lower bound value of 2 and an upper bound value of 6. The random number stream is set to 1 (figure 6.22). Repeat this procedure for the part002 element giving it a name of cutomer2arrivals, a first arrival time and interarrival time of Gamma (1,10,1) and setting the processtime attribute to UNIFORM(4,10,1). Next double click on the buffer001 element and enter queue1 in the name field.

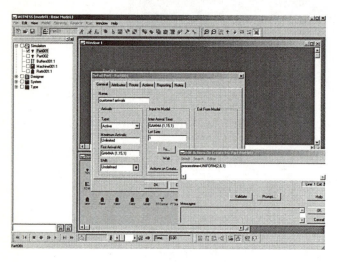

Figure 6.22 Entering the part detail information

The next step is to define the machine detail information. Double-click on the machine001 element and enter bankclerk in the name field. Enter 2 in the capacity field and processtime in the cycle time field (figure 6.23).

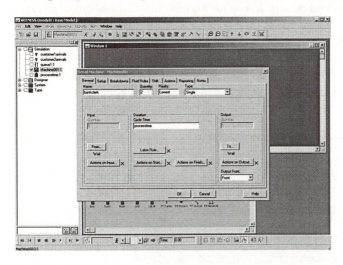

Figure 6.23 Entering the machine detail information

Simulation Modelling for Business

The next step before we can run the model is to connect the elements to define the routes for the entity (customer) flow. Click on the customer1arrivals part element and click on the visual push button ($\mathscr{A}$) located on the standard action bar. The output rule for customer1arrivals window should be displayed (figure 6.24). Click on the queue1 element to observe the rule PUSH queue1(1). This directs entities (customers) from the customer1arrivals element to the queue1 element. Click on OK to close the window. Repeat the operation for the customer2arrivals element. Click on the element, click on the visual push button and then click on the queue1 icon. This will direct customer2arrivals to the queue1 element also.

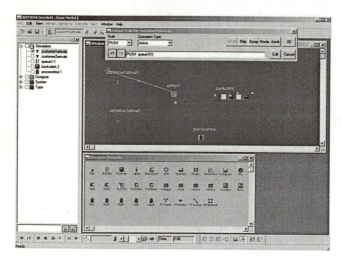

Figure 6.24 Entering the part detail rule information

Click on the bankclerk machine element and then click on the visual pull button (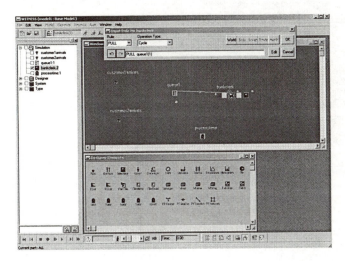) located on the standard action bar. The output rule for the bankclerk machine should be displayed (figure 6.25). Click on the queue1 element to observe the rule PULL queue1(1). This directs entities (customers) from the queue1 element to the bankclerk machine element when capacity becomes available. Click OK and then click on the bankclerk element to select it. Then click on the visual push button. Click on the SHIP button in the output rule for bankclerk window to observe the rule PUSH SHIP. This directs entities which have been processed at the bank clerk out of the simulation. Click OK to close the window.

Figure 6.25 Entering the machine detail rule information

Set the time for the end of the run in the text box next to the run until button (alarm clock symbol) on the run toolbar by clicking in the box and typing in 480. Now click on the run button (▶) to run the simulation. To obtain statistics click on the relevant element in the simulation window and then click on the statistics report icon in the reporting toolbar. (If any toolbar is not visible go to the view toolbars menu option to make the toolbar visible). Figure 6.26 shows the report generated when clicking on the queue1 element and then the reporting icon.

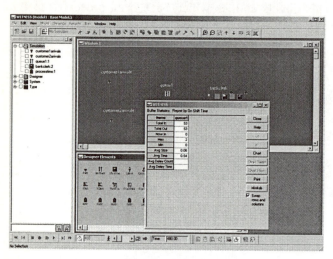

Figure 6.26 Queue report screen

In order to provide the statistics required (i.e. minimum, average and maximum customer time in the system) it is necessary to add additional elements to the simulation screen. Add a histogram element (name it hist1), a real number attribute (Rattr) element (name it arrivaltime) and three real number variables (vreal) elements (name them timeinsys, mintime and maxtime). See figure 6.27 for the updated simulation screen.

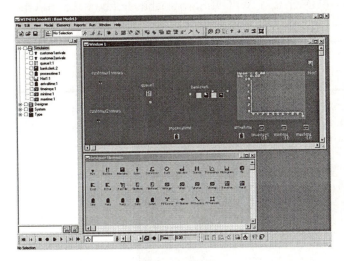

Figure 6.27 Entering the histogram and results variables

In order to record the time in system for customers it is necessary to record the arrival and leave times of each entity (customer) and collate these to calculate the minimum, average and maximum time in system values. To achieve this double click on the customer1arrivals elements and click on the 'Actions on Create' button. In addition to the current processtime assignment add another line arrivaltime=TIME. This saves the time of entry of the entity (TIME is a WITNESS variable holding the current simulation time) in the part attribute arrivaltime. Close the window and click on the 'Actions on Leave' button. Type timeinsys=TIME-arrivaltime, to enter the time in system for the current entity in the variable timeinsys. Enter a further line RECORD timeinsys in Hist1. This saves the variable timeinsys in the Hist1 histogram element. Enter the lines mintime=HMIN(Hist1) and maxtime=HMAX(Hist1) to record the minimum and maximum time in system values (figure 6.28). Repeat the above for the customer2arrivals element.

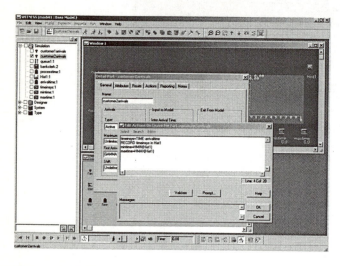

Figure 6.28 Entering the part leave actions

Run the simulation again by resetting the time to zero using the reset button
(◄◄) on the run toolbar and then click on the run button. The results are
shown in figure 6.29. In this case the average time in the system for a
customer (from the histogram display) is given as 6.27 minutes, with a
minimum time of 2.3 minutes and a maximum time of 11.9 minutes. The
value for the timeinsys variable is the time in system for the last customer
to leave the simulation before the run has been stopped and is ignored for
reporting purposes.

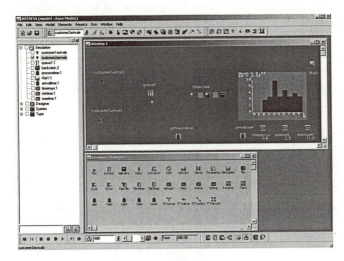

Figure 6.29 Bank clerk simulation results

The Dual Queue Bank Clerk Simulation

In most systems decisions are made which require modelling. A model incorporating a decision will be demonstrated by extending the bank clerk simulation previously developed. In this version of the bank clerk simulation there are two bank clerks available. On entry to the bank the customer has a choice of bank clerk so it will be assumed that they will pick the bank clerk with the queue containing the smallest number of waiting customers. The above scenarios can be represented with a process map as follows (figure 6.30).

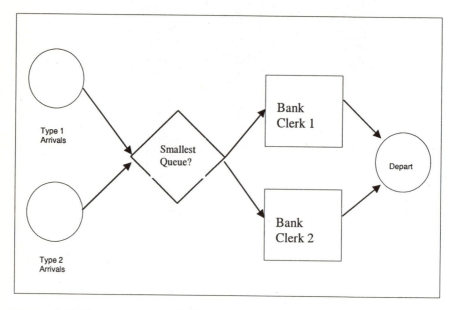

Figure 6.30 Process map of decision-based bank clerk simulation

Building the Model using ARENA

To implement the dual queue system use the single queue model and make the following changes. Delete the connecting lines between the assign modules and the process block by clicking on the lines and pressing the Del key on the keyboard. Add a further process module and a decide module. Click on the connect button ⬛ on the toolbar and connect the additional modules as shown in figure 6.31.

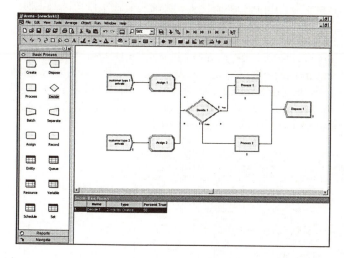

Figure 6.31 Adding the decide and process modules

The next step is to define the parameters of the two modules placed on the screen. Double click on the decide module and select 2-way by condition as the type parameter. For the If parameter select Expression. For the value parameter enter the following expression (figure 6.32).

NQ(bank clerk 1.Queue).LT.NQ(bank clerk 2.Queue)

This expression demonstrates the use of a conditional logic statement in ARENA. Decisions can be represented by either an IF...THEN...ELSE conditional formula or a probability formula using the by Chance option. In this case the formula compares the number of customers in the queue for bank clerk 1 and if this is less than the number in the bank clerk 2 queue the condition is TRUE and the entity/customer leaves the decide module on the TRUE route. Otherwise the entity/customer leaves on the FALSE route. In this case the TRUE route should connect to process 1 (bank clerk 1) and the FALSE route will connect to process 2 (bank clerk 2).

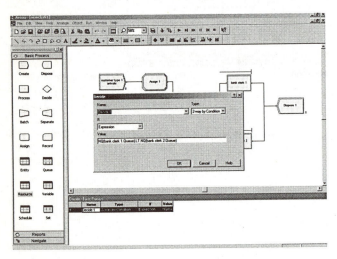

Figure 6.32 Entering the decide module parameters

Finally double click on the process 2 module, select the seize/delay/release option for action and add the resource bank clerk with a quantity of 1 (figure 6.33).

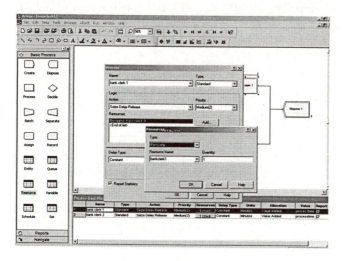

Figure 6.33 Entering the process 2 parameters

Run the simulation by clicking on the run (▶) button on the toolbar. When the simulation has completed the results screen will be displayed as in figure 6.34. The total customer time in system is given as an average of 7.63 minutes, with a minimum of 2.01 minutes and a maximum of 17.31 minutes (figure 6.34).

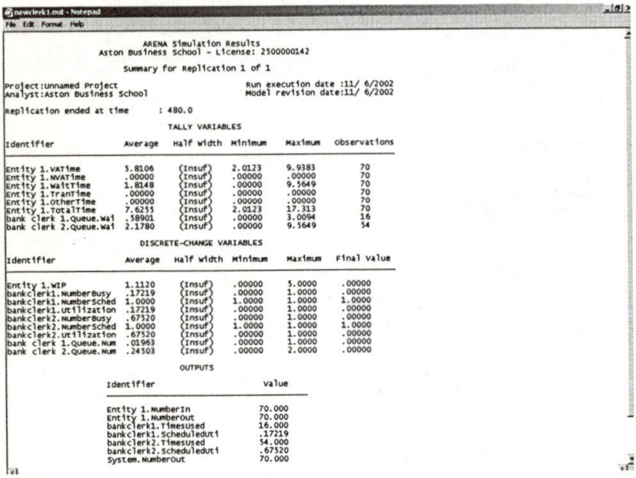

```
 newclerk1.out - Notepad                                                    _|8|x

File  Edit  Format  Help

                        ARENA Simulation Results
                  Aston Business School - License: 2500000142

                        Summary for Replication 1 of 1

Project:unnamed Project                      Run execution date :11/ 6/2002
Analyst:Aston Business School                Model revision date:11/ 6/2002

Replication ended at time       : 480.0

                             TALLY VARIABLES

Identifier           Average   Half width   Minimum    Maximum   Observations

Entity 1.VATime      5.8106    (Insuf)      2.0123     9.9383        70
Entity 1.NVATime      .00000   (Insuf)       .00000     .00000       70
Entity 1.WaitTime    1.8148    (Insuf)       .00000    9.5649        70
Entity 1.TranTime     .00000   (Insuf)       .00000     .00000       70
Entity 1.OtherTime    .00000   (Insuf)       .00000     .00000       70
Entity 1.TotalTime   7.6255    (Insuf)      2.0123    17.313         70
bank clerk 1.Queue.Wai .58901  (Insuf)       .00000    3.0094        16
bank clerk 2.Queue.Wai 2.1780  (Insuf)       .00000    9.5649        54

                        DISCRETE-CHANGE VARIABLES

Identifier           Average   Half width   Minimum    Maximum   Final Value

Entity 1.WIP         1.1120    (Insuf)       .00000    5.0000     .00000
bankclerk1.NumberBusy .17219   (Insuf)       .00000    1.0000     .00000
bankclerk1.NumberSched 1.0000  (Insuf)      1.0000     1.0000    1.0000
bankclerk1.Utilization .17219  (Insuf)       .00000    1.0000     .00000
bankclerk2.NumberBusy .67520   (Insuf)       .00000    1.0000     .00000
bankclerk2.NumberSched 1.0000  (Insuf)      1.0000     1.0000    1.0000
bankclerk2.Utilization .67520  (Insuf)       .00000    1.0000     .00000
bank clerk 1.Queue.Num .01963  (Insuf)       .00000    1.0000     .00000
bank clerk 2.Queue.Num .24503  (Insuf)       .00000    2.0000     .00000

                              OUTPUTS

              Identifier                    Value

              Entity 1.NumberIn             70.000
              Entity 1.NumberOut            70.000
              bankclerk1.TimesUsed          16.000
              bankclerk1.ScheduledUti        .17219
              bankclerk2.TimesUsed          54.000
              bankclerk2.ScheduledUti        .67520
              System.NumberOut              70.000
```

Figure 6.34 Results screen for ARENA dual queue model

Building the Model using SIMUL8

To implement the dual queue system we must first add an additional storage area to the screen by clicking on the relevant option (🖫) on the toolbar. We then need to add entity flow routes from the work entry points to the new storage areas. To do this click on the route drawing mode button (✍) on the toolbar, then click on the work entry point 1 icon. Then click on storage area 2. Then add another route from work entry point 2 to storage area 2. Routing lines will be added as in figure 6.35.

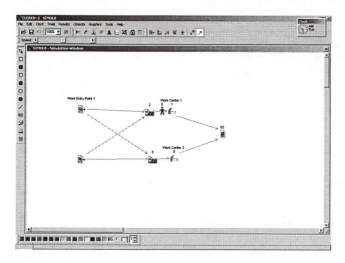

Figure 6.35 Adding routing information for bank clerk simulation

Next it is necessary to set the rule for choosing which work centre the customers will use after entering the system at the work entry points. In this case the decision rule is based on the work centre with the shortest queue of customers. In order to achieve this double click on work entry point 1 and click on the routing out button. Click on the shortest queue button (figure 6.36). Repeat the same for work entry point 2.

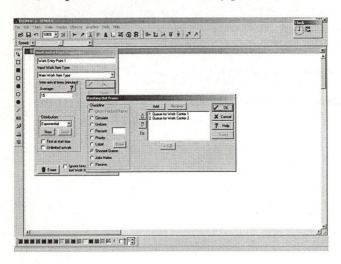

Figure 6.36 Setting rules for queue choice

Next run the simulation and observe the results (figure 6.37). The results show an average customer time in the system of 7.85 minutes, with a minimum time of 2.36 minutes and a maximum time of 21.78 minutes.

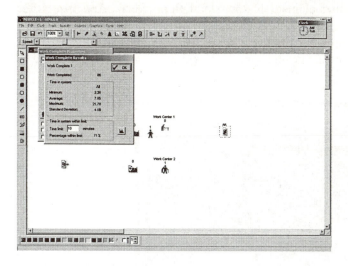

Figure 6.37 SIMUL8 results for dual queue system

Building the Model using WITNESS

To implement the dual queue system we must first add an additional buffer element and machine element to the simulation screen. Add the buffer element and name it queue2. Add the machine element, name it bankclerk2 and enter processtime for the cycle time. Rename the bankclerk element bankclerk1 and change its capacity to 1. The simulation screen should be as figure 6.38.

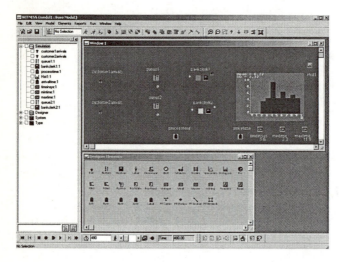

Figure 6.38 Adding elements for dual queue bank clerk simulation

The next step is to connect the elements to make a dual queue model. Double click on the customer1arrivals element and click on the visual push button on the standard action bar. Click on the edit button and enter the following (see also figure 6.39):

IF NPARTS(queue1) < NPARTS(queue2)
 PUSH to queue1
ELSE
 PUSH to queue2
ENDIF

This statement uses the WITNESS function NPARTS which gives the number of entities in the named queue. Thus if there are less entities in queue1 than queue2 then move this entity to queue1, otherwise move the entity to queue2. Enter the same expression for the customer2arrivals element. Now define the routing for the bank clerk machine elements. For the bankclerk1 element define the input rule PULL queue1 and the output rule PUSH SHIP. For the bankclerk2 element define the input rule PULL queue2 and the output rule PUSH SHIP.

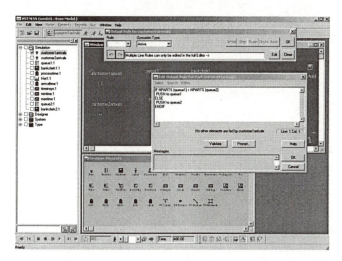

Figure 6.39 Adding part detail rule information

Run the simulation again by resetting the time to zero using the reset button
(◄◄) on the run toolbar and then click on the run button. The results are
shown in figure 6.40. In this case the average time in the system for a
customer (from the histogram display) is given as 7.37 minutes, with a
minimum time of 2.1 minutes and a maximum time of 14.5 minutes.

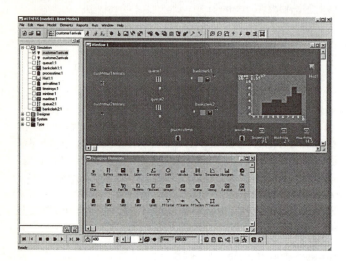

Figure 6.40 WITNESS results for dual queue simulation

Summary

The model building stage can be undertaken using a general purpose computer language, a simulation language or a visual interactive modelling system (VIM). This chapter has shown the use of the ARENA, SIMUL8 and WITNESS visual interactive modelling systems to build a simple simulation model.

Exercises

6.1. Using a simulation system simulate the following two types of customer arrive at a system for processing. Type 1 customers arrive according to an exponential interarrival distribution with a mean of ten minutes. These customers wait in a dedicated queue (for type 1 customers) until an operator is ready to process them. The processing time is a triangular distribution with parameters of five, six and eight minutes. Type 2 customers arrive according to an exponential distribution with a mean of 15 minutes. These customers wait in a dedicated queue (for type 2 customers) until an operator is ready to process them. The processing time is a triangular distribution with parameters of three, seven and eight minutes. All customers then go through a further operation with a processing time distribution that is triangular with parameters of four, six and eight minutes. Customers then leave the system. Assuming transfer times between operations is negligible, determine the average time in system for each customer type and the average queue size for each operation.

6.2. Using a simulation system simulate the following: parts arrive at a single machine according to an exponential interarrival distribution with a mean of 15 minutes. The processing time is a triangular distribution with parameters of 10, 14, 17 minutes. Each part has then a ten per cent chance of being inspected for quality. The inspection time is given by a normal distribution with a mean of 100 minutes and a standard deviation of ten minutes. About 15 per cent of the inspected parts fail the quality test and are scrapped. The remaining parts join the non-inspected parts and are transferred out of the system. Run the simulation for 10,000 minutes to determine the number of inspected parts, the number of scrap parts and the total number of parts that leave the system.

6.3. A harbour consists of four docks for unloading and loading ships. Ships arrive at the harbour with an interarrival time of five hours with an exponential distribution. Ships unload at the first available dock with a normal distribution with a mean duration of six hours and a standard deviation of 24 hours. Ships then load immediately (with a normal distribution with a mean of eight hours and a standard deviation of three hours) and immediately leave the harbour. Build a simulation model to estimate the utilisation of the four harbour docks and the maximum time a ship is required to wait for an available dock.

6.4. A university car park has a staff car park holding 100 vehicles and a student car park holding 50 vehicles. Staff arrive during the day with an interarrival rate given by an exponential distribution with a mean of ten minutes. Staff stay on campus for an average of four hours and then leave. The students' interarrival rate is described by an exponential distribution with a mean of 15 minutes. Students stay on campus for an average of three hours. Run the simulation for five days and note the length of time when the car park is full during this time. Discuss changes to the model to make it a more realistic representation of a typical car park system.

Chapter 7

Validation and Verification

Introduction

Before experimental analysis of the simulation model can begin it is necessary to ensure that the model constructed provides a valid representation of the system we are studying. This process consists of verification and validation of the simulation model. Verification refers to ensuring that the computer model built using the simulation software is a correct representation of the process map of the system under investigation. Validation concerns ensuring that the assumptions made in the process map about the real-world system are acceptable in the context of the simulation study. Both topics will now be discussed in more detail.

Verification

Verification is analogous to the practice of 'debugging' a computer program. Thus many of the following techniques will be familiar to programmers of general-purpose computer languages.

Model Design

The task of verification is likely to become greater with an increase in model size. This is because a large complex program is both more likely to contain errors and these errors are less likely to be found. Due to this behaviour most practitioners advise on an approach of building a small simple model, ensuring that this works correctly, and then gradually adding embellishments over time. This approach is intended to help limit the area of search for errors at any one time. It is also important to ensure that unnecessary complexity is not incorporated in the model design. The design should incorporate only enough detail to ensure the study objectives and not attempt to be an exact replica of the real-life system.

Structured Walkthrough

This enables the modeller to incorporate the perspective of someone outside the immediate task of model construction. The walkthrough procedure involves talking through the program code with another individual or team. The process may bring fresh insight from others, but the act of explaining the coding can also help the person who has developed the code discover their own errors. In discrete-event simulation code is executed non-sequentially and different coding blocks are executing simultaneously. This means that the walkthrough may best be conducted by following the 'life-history' of an entity through the simulation coding, rather than a sequential examination of coding blocks.

Test Runs

Test runs of a simulation model can be made during program development to check model behaviour. This is a useful way of checking model behaviour as a defective model will usually report results (e.g. machine utilisation, customer wait times) which do not conform to expectations, either based on the real system performance or common sense deductions. It may be necessary to add performance measures to the model (e.g. costs) for verification purposes, even though they may not be required for reporting purposes. One approach is to use historical (fixed) data, so model behaviour can be isolated from behaviour caused by the use of random variates in the model. It is also important to test model behaviour under a number of scenarios, particularly boundary conditions that are likely to uncover erratic behaviour. Boundary conditions could include minimum and maximum arrival rates, minimum and maximum service times and minimum and maximum rate of infrequent events (e.g. machine breakdowns).

Trace Analysis

Due to the nature of discrete-event simulation it may be difficult to locate the source of a coding error. Most simulation packages incorporate an entity trace facility that is useful in providing a detailed record of the life-history of a particular entity. The trace facility can show the events occurring for a particular entity or all events occurring during a particular time frame. The trace analysis facility can produce a large amount of output so it is most often used for detailed verification.

Animation Inspection

The animation facilities of simulation software packages provide a powerful tool in aiding understanding of model behaviour. The animation enables the model developer to see many of the model components and their behaviour simultaneously. A 'rough-cut' animated drawing should be sufficient at the testing stage for verification purposes. To aid understanding, model components can be animated which may not appear in the final layout presented to a client. The usefulness of the animation technique will be maximised if the animation software facilities permit reliable and quick production of the animation effects.

Documentation

It is important to document all elements in the simulation to aid verification by other personnel or at a later date. Any general purpose or simulation coding should have comments attached to each line of code. Each object within a model produced on a visual interactive modelling system requires comments regarding its purpose and details of parameters and other elements.

Verification with ARENA

As an example of verification with a visual interactive modelling system, this section examines verification using the ARENA software. ARENA provides a number of facilities for model verification. Animation facilities provide immediate feedback to the user from which the model logic can be checked by following the path of entities through the animated display. Errors can also be found by inspecting the measure of performance (e.g. machine utilisation, queue length) within the system and comparing them to estimated values made through the use of rough-cut calculations. In testing both the model logic and performance, particular attention should be paid to any behaviour at variance from the real system (taking into consideration simplifying assumptions made) or expected behaviour of a system that does not yet exist. As was stated earlier verification is easiest with small simple models. With larger and more complex models it may be necessary to temporarily simplify model behaviour for verification purposes. This could be achieved through replacing distributions for arrival and process times with constant values or only routing one entity type through the model to check the entity path. If the model is not behaving in an appropriate manner it is necessary to investigate the model design. This can be achieved through inspection of the model code and by analysing the event calendar using the debugging facilities.

ARENA converts the module specification you have placed in the model window into the simulation language SIMAN. This consists of a model file containing the simulation logic modules and an experimental file containing the data modules. To view these files for a simulation select

the Run/SIMAN/View option. The SIMAN files for the bank clerk
simulation is shown in figure 7.1 and figure 7.2.

```
;
;
;      Model statements for module:  Arrive 1
;
42$           CREATE,      1:EXPO(15):MARK(arrivaltime);
43$           ASSIGN:      customertype=1:
                           processtime=UNIFORM(2,6);
3$            STATION,     Arrive 1;
51$           TRACE,       -1,"-Arrived to system at station Arrive
1\n":;
6$            ASSIGN:      Picture=Default;
27$           DELAY:       0.;
56$           TRACE,       -1,"-Transferred to station Server 1\n":;
29$           ROUTE:       1,Server 1;
;
;
;      Model statements for module:  Arrive 2
;
121$          CREATE,      1:EXPO(10):MARK(arrivaltime);
122$          ASSIGN:      customertype=2:
                           processtime=UNIFORM(4,10);
82$           STATION,     Arrive 2;
130$          TRACE,       -1,"-Arrived to system at station Arrive
2\n":;
85$           ASSIGN:      Picture=Default;
106$          DELAY:       0.;
135$          TRACE,       -1,"-Transferred to station Server 1\n":;
108$          ROUTE:       1,Server 1;
;
;
;      Model statements for module:  Server 1
;
0$            STATION,     Server 1;
237$          TRACE,       -1,"-Arrived to station Server 1\n":;
200$          DELAY:       0.;
244$          TRACE,       -1,"-Waiting for resource Server 1_R\n":;
161$          QUEUE,       Server 1_R_Q:MARK(QueueTime);
162$          SEIZE,       1:
                           Server 1_R,1;
271$          BRANCH,      1:
                           If,RTYP(Server 1_R).eq.2,272$,Yes:
                           If,RTYP(Server 1_R).eq.1,174$,Yes;
272$          MOVE:        Server 1_R,Server 1;
174$          TALLY:       Server 1_R_Q Queue Time,INT(QueueTime),1;
281$          DELAY:       0.0;
              TRACE,   -1,"-Delay for processing time processtime\n":;
163$          DELAY:       processtime;
245$          TRACE,       -1,"-Releasing resource\n":;
164$          RELEASE:     Server 1_R,1;
228$          DELAY:       0.;
250$          TRACE,       -1,"-Transferred to station Depart 1\n":;
168$          ROUTE:       1,Depart 1;
;
;
;      Model statements for module:  Depart 1
;
2$            STATION,     Depart 1;
```

```
312$        TRACE,           -1,"-Arrived to station Depart 1\n":;
282$        DELAY:           0.;
305$        COUNT:           counterset(customertype),1;
309$        TALLY:           service time,Interval(arrivaltime),1;
319$        TRACE,           -1,"-Disposing entity\n":;
311$        DISPOSE;
```

Figure 7.1 ARENA model listing

```
PROJECT,        ;
ATTRIBUTES:     arrivaltime:
                customertype:
                processtime:
                QueueTime;
QUEUES:         Server 1_R_Q,FIFO;
PICTURES:       Default;
RESOURCES:      Server 1_R,Capacity(1,),-,Stationary;
STATIONS:       Arrive 1:
                Arrive 2:
                Depart 1:
                Server 1;
COUNTERS:       customer type 1:
                customer type 2;
TALLIES:        service time:
                Server 1_R_Q Queue Time;
DSTATS:         NQ(Server 1_R_Q),# in Server 1_R_Q:
                MR(Server 1_R),Server 1_R Available:
                NR(Server 1_R),Server 1_R Busy;
REPLICATE,      1,0.0,1000,Yes,Yes;
SETS:           counterset,customer type 1,customer type 2;
```

Figure 7.2 ARENA experimental listing

These files are of course most useful if you are familiar with the SIMAN simulation language. Note also the coding in the model listing (figure 7.1) does not necessarily follow the sequence of modules in the order of the model logic. Unfortunately edited code cannot be converted back to an ARENA program so SIMAN code is restricted to being an aid for verification. Also debugging from a code listing is more difficult than for a general purpose language such as C, as many parts of the model can be executing simultaneously as many entities are passing through the model at any one time. To inspect the actions of each entity an event debugger is required. The debugging facilities are available in the ARENA run controller which provides a number of facilities for inspecting model behaviour. The run controller is activated by the Run/Command menu option or the command button on the Run interaction toolbar. When activated a window is opened and a prompt will appear. The SET TRACE command is used to provide a visual display of all the simulation events. Figure 7.3 shows the debugger used to provide a trace of the first ten lines of code.

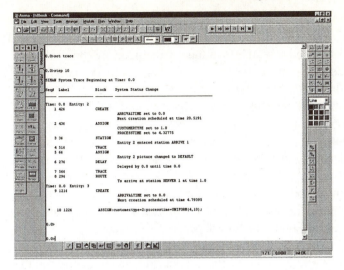

Figure 7.3 ARENA trace listing

Figure 7.4 shows the trace cancel option disabled and the use of the show command to find the number of customers in the server 1 queue. The view command is then shown the attributes of the entities in the server 1 queue.

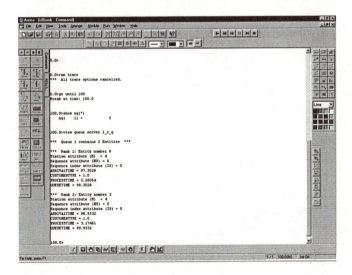

Figure 7.4 ARENA debugger display

Validation

A verified model is a model which operates as intended by the modeller. However this does not necessarily mean that it is a satisfactory representation of the real system for the purposes of the study. Validation is about ensuring that model behaviour is close enough to the real-world system for the purposes of the simulation study. Unlike verification, the question of validation is one of judgement. Ideally the model should provide enough accuracy for the measures required whilst limiting the amount of effort required to achieve this. For most systems of any complexity this aim can be achieved in a number of ways and a key skill of the simulation developer is finding the most efficient way of achieving this goal. Pegden et al. (1995) outlines three aspects of validation:

- Conceptual Validity – Does the model adequately represent the real-world system?
- Operational Validity – Are the model generated behavioural data characteristic of the real-world system behavioural data?
- Believability – Does the simulation model's ultimate user have confidence in the model's results?

Conceptual Validity

Conceptual validation involves ensuring that the model structure and elements are correctly chosen and configured in order to adequately represent the real-world system. As we know that the model is a simplification of the real world then there is a need for a consensus around the form of the conceptual model between the model builder and the user. To ensure a credible model is produced the model builder should discuss and obtain information from people familiar with the real-world system including operating personnel, industrial engineers, management, vendors and documentation. They should also observe system behaviour over time and compare with model behaviour and communicate with project sponsors throughout the model build to increase credibility.

Operational Validity

This involves ensuring that the results obtained from the model are consistent with real-world performance. A common way of ensuring operational validity is to use the technique of sensitivity analysis to test the behaviour of the model under various scenarios and compare results with real-world behaviour. The technique of common random numbers can be used to isolate changes due to random variation. The techniques of experimental design can also be employed to conduct sensitivity analysis over two or more factors. Note that for validation purposes these tests are comparing simulation performance with real-world performance while in the context of experimentation they are used to compare simulation behaviour under different scenarios.

Sensitivity analysis can be used to validate a model but it is particularly appropriate if a model has been built of a system which does not exist as the data has been estimated and cannot be validated against a real system. In this case the main task is to determine the effect of variation in this data on model results. If there is little variation in output as a consequence of a change in input then we can be reasonably confident in the results. It should also be noted that an option may be to conduct sensitivity analysis on sub-systems of the overall system being modelled which do exist. This emphasises the point that the model should be robust enough to provide a prediction of what would happen in the real system under a range of possible input data. The construction and validation of the model should be for a particular range of input values defined in the simulation project objectives. If the simulation is then used outside of this predefined range the model must be re-validated to ensure additional aspects of the real system are incorporated to ensure valid results.

An alternative to comparing the output of the simulation to a real system output is to use actual historical data in the model, rather than derive a probability distribution. Data collected could be used for elements such as customer arrival times and service delays. By comparing output measures across identical time periods it should be possible to validate the model. Thus the structure or flow of the model could be validated and then probability distributions entered for random elements. Thus any error in system performance could be identified as either a logic error or from an inaccurate distribution. The disadvantage of this method is that for a model of any size the amount of historical data needed will be substantial. It is also necessary to read this data, either from a file or array, requiring additional coding effort.

Sensitivity analysis should be undertaken by observing the output measure of interest with data set to levels above and below the initial set level for the data. A graph may be used to show model results for a range of data values if detailed analysis is required (e.g. a non-linear relationship between a data value and output measure is apparent). If the model output does not show a significant change in value in response to the sensitivity analysis then we can judge that the accuracy of the estimated value will not have a significant effect on the result.

If the model output is sensitive to the data value then preferably we would want to increase the accuracy of the data value estimate. This may be undertaken by further interviews or data collection. In any event the simulation analysis will need to show the effect of model output on a range of data values. Thus for an estimated value we can observe the likely behaviour of the system over a range of data values within which the true value should be located. Further sensitivity analysis may be required on each of these values to separate changes in output values from random variation.

When it is found that more than one data value has an effect on an output measure, then the effects of the individual and combined data values should be assessed. This will require 3^k replications to measure the minimum, initial and maximum values for k variables. The use of fractional factorial designs techniques (Law and Kelton, 2000) may be used to reduce the number of replications required.

Believability

In order to ensure implementation of actions recommended as a result of simulation experiments, the model output must be seen as credible from the simulation user's point of view. This credibility will be enhanced by close co-operation between model user and client throughout the simulation study. This involves agreeing clear project objectives explaining the capabilities of the technique to the client and agreeing assumptions made in the process map. Regular meetings of interested parties, using the simulation animation display to provide a discussion forum, can increase confidence in model results. Believability emphasises how there is no one answer to achieving model validity and the perspective of both users and developers that a model is valid needs to be satisfied.

Summary

Verification aims to ensure that the model built is a correct representation of the system process map. Techniques used to achieve this include model design, using small and simple models, a structured walkthrough of the model code, test runs, trace analysis and inspection of the computer animation.

Validation aims to ensure that model behaviour is close enough to the real-world system for the objectives of the simulation study. Conceptual validity aims to ensure that the model structure is correct and operational validity aims to ensure model results are consistent with real-world behaviour. Finally the model has to have credibility from the viewpoint of the model user.

Sensitivity analysis can be used to investigate model behaviour as input data values are changed. This can be compared to real-world behaviour or, if no real-world system exists, used to identify variables which have a significant effect on system behaviour.

Exercises

7.1. Distinguish between the techniques of verification and validation.

7.2. Search for papers on the web site www.informs-cs.org/wscpapers.html and discuss methods used by practitioners for verification and validation.

7.3. How would you ensure conceptual validity, operational validity and believability?

7.4. Discuss the role of sensitivity analysis in validation.

Chapter 8

Experimentation and Analysis

Introduction

The stochastic nature of simulation means that when a simulation is run the performance measures generated are a sample from a random distribution. Thus each simulation 'run' will generate a different result, derived from the randomness which has been modelled. In order to interpret the results (i.e. separate the random changes in output from changes in performance) statistical procedures are outlined in this chapter which are used for the analysis of the results of runs of a simulation. There are two types of simulation system that need to be defined, each requiring different methods of data analysis.

Terminating Systems

These run between pre-defined states or times where the end state matches the initial state of the simulation. For example a simulation of a shop from opening to closing time.

Non-Terminating Systems

These do not reach pre-defined states or times. In particular the initial state is not returned to, for example a manufacturing facility.

Most service organisations tend to be terminating systems which close at the end of each day with no in-process inventory (i.e. people waiting for service) and thus return to the 'empty' or 'idle' state they had at the start of that day. Most manufacturing organisations are non-terminating with inventory in the system that is awaiting a process. Thus even if the facility shuts down temporarily it will start again in a different state to the previous start-state (i.e. the inventory levels define different starting conditions). However the same system may be classified as terminating or non-terminating depending on the objectives of the study. Before a non-terminating system is analysed the bias introduced by the non-representative starting conditions must be eliminated to obtain what are termed steady-state conditions from which a representative statistical analysis can be undertaken.

Statistical Analysis for Terminating Systems

This section will provide statistical tools to analyse either terminating systems or the steady-state phase of non-terminating systems. The statistics relevant to both the analysis of a single model and comparison between different models will now be outlined in turn.

Single Model Statistical Analysis

The output measure of a simulation model is a random variable and so we need to conduct multiple runs (replications) of the model to provide us with a sample of its value. When a number of replications have been undertaken the sample mean can be calculated by averaging the measure of interest (e.g. time in queue) over the number of replications made. Each replication will use a different set of random numbers and so this procedure is called the method of independent replications.

Establishing a Confidence Interval

To assess the precision of our results we can compute a confidence interval or range around the sample mean that will include, to a certain level of confidence, the true mean value of the variable we are measuring. Thus confidence intervals provide a point estimate of the expected average (average over infinite number of replications) and an idea of how precise this estimate is. The confidence interval will fall as replications increase. Thus a confidence interval does not mean that say 95 per cent of values fall within this interval, but that we are 95 per cent sure that the interval contains the expected average.

For large samples (replications) of over around 50 the normal distribution can be used for the computations. However the sample size for a simulation experiment will normally be less than this with ten replications of a simulation being common. In this case, provided the population is approximately normally distributed, the sampling distribution follows a t-distribution. The formula for the confidence interval involving the t-distribution is as follows:

$$\mu = \overline{x} \pm \frac{t * s}{\sqrt{n}}$$

where

μ = true (population) mean

x̄ = sample mean

t = t-distribution value

s = standard deviation

n = sample size

Both the confidence interval analysis and the t-tests presented later for comparison analysis assume the data measured is normally distributed. This assumption is usually acceptable if measuring an average value for each replication as the output variable is made from many measurements and the central limit theorem applies. However the central limit theorem applies for a large sample size, and the definition of what constitutes a large sample depends partly on how close the actual distribution of the output variable is to the normal distribution. A histogram can be used to observe how close the actual distribution is to the normal distribution curve.

Confidence interval analysis will be demonstrated using the EXCEL spreadsheet and the ARENA and SIMUL8 simulation software.

Confidence Interval Analysis using EXCEL

A confidence interval analysis can be easily conducted using an EXCEL spreadsheet as in figure 8.1. The t-distribution value which requires the significance level (say 0.05) and degrees of freedom (sample size–1) value is calculated using the EXCEL function TINV. In this case the parameters 0.05 and 9 are used. The standard deviation is calculated using the STDEV function. The sample size is simply entered as the number of replications, in this case 20. Figure 8.1 shows the spreadsheet which provides confidence intervals for the dual queue average time in system and single queue average time in system over 20 replications based on the ARENA simulation results of the model developed in figure 8.4.

	A	B	C	D
1	Replication	Dual Queue Average Time in System	Single Queue Average Time in System	
2	1	7.21	5.97	
3	2	8.07	6.66	
4	3	7.35	6	
5	4	8.08	6.74	
6	5	7.03	5.68	
7	6	7.78	6.35	
8	7	7.51	6.07	
9	8	7.31	5.66	
10	9	7.3	6.3	
11	10	7.12	6.14	
12	11	7.71	6.5	
13	12	8.44	7.01	
14	13	9.62	8.43	
16	15	7.82	6.37	
17	16	8.19	7.01	
18	17	7.08	5.8	
19	18	8.81	7.7	
20	19	7.99	6.66	
21	20	6.96	5.31	formulae for bank clerk 1
22	Average	7.84	6.54	=AVERAGE(B2:B21)
23	Standard Deviation	0.77	0.85	=STDEV(b2:b21)
24	t value (a–0.05)	2.09	2.09	=TINV(0.05,b25-1)
25	sample size	20.00	20.00	=COUNT(b2:b21)
26	half width	0.36	0.40	=(B24*B23)/SQRT(B25)
27	upper	8.21	6.93	=+B22+B26
28	lower	7.48	6.14	=+B22-B26

Figure 8.1 Confidence interval analysis using EXCEL

The results show that we can be 95 per cent confident that the dual queue average time in system is between 7.48 and 8.21 minutes and the single queue average time in system is between 6.14 and 6.93 minutes.

Confidence Interval Analysis using ARENA

ARENA can be used to analyse the bank clerk simulation constructed in chapter 6. Before the analysis can begin however an adjustment to the code must be made to ensure the simulation is a true terminating system. At present the simulation starts from empty and then customers arrive at the bank with a run-time specified of 480 minutes. To be a true terminating system the simulation must reach its starting condition (i.e. empty system) at the end of its run. To achieve this, the simulation must stop receiving new customers after a certain time period and then service any remaining customers in the system. One method of achieving this is to add an additional condition to the ARENA decide module which directs all customers after 'closing time' away from the bank. To update the bank clerk simulation to a terminating system load the dual queue bank clerk simulation into ARENA (see chapter 5). Double click on the Decide module and copy the current queue select expression onto the clipboard by dragging the mouse over it and selecting on the edit/copy menu option. Change the type field from 2-way by condition to n-way by condition. Click on the add button and enter the expression TNOW.GT.480 (figure 8.2). TNOW is an ARENA variable containing the current simulation time. This command will redirect customers to a dispose module if the current time is greater than 480 minutes. Click on the add button again and select expression for the If field and paste the queue select expression to the value field by clicking on the field and selecting the menu/paste option.

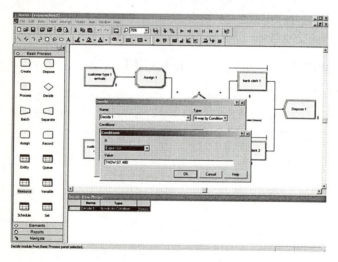

Figure 8.2 Entering the Decide module parameters

Click on the dispose module and click on the model window to add the module. Use the connect button on the toolbar to connect the two modules. Also use the connect button to connect the queue select option to the bank clerk 1 module. The simulation should be as in figure 8.3.

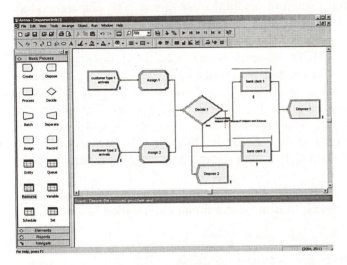

Figure 8.3 Entering the module connections

Select the run/setup/replication option from the menu. Enter 510 for the run length to provide 30 minutes for customers to leave the system after the closing time at 480 minutes. Enter 20 for the 'Number of Replications' parameter and ensure the tick boxes in the 'initialize between replications' area are checked for 'System' and 'Statistics' to achieve statistically independent replications.

150 Simulation Modelling for Business

In order to save information to a data file for analysis we use the outputs module from the elements template. To use the elements template click on the template attach icon on the toolbar and select the elements template file. Click on the outputs module and drag on to the simulation window. Double click on the outputs module to obtain the dialog box. The outputs module allows statistics to be saved to a data file which can be analysed by the ARENA Output Analyzer. The output analyzer is a program which is supplied with the ARENA system (it may need to be installed and run separately from the main ARENA system). To collect statistics on the average time in system, type entity 1.totaltime in the SIMAN expression field. Enter the output file as "BCD.DAT" (with quotes). Enter the name dual queue average time in system (figure 8.4). Run (fast-forward) the model, the animation facilities should be disabled and the model run will quickly complete. The file holding the time in system information will be created.

Repeat the above changes to the single queue system (see figures 8.2, 8.3, 8.4) and save the time in system timings to the file BCS.DAT.

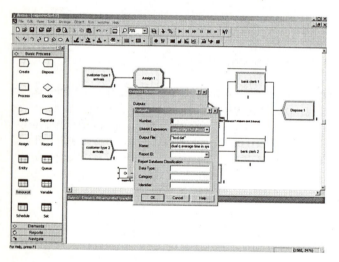

Figure 8.4 Entering the outputs module parameters

The next step is to use the output analyzer to perform the statistical analysis. Run the program and select the Analyse/Confidence Interval on Mean/Classical menu option. Add the file BCD.DAT and select 'lumped' from the pull-down menu for the replications parameter. Data from the 20 replications are now presented together to compute the confidence interval. Click on OK. Add the file BCS.DAT. Select 'lumped' from the pull-down menu for the replications parameter. Click on OK. Leave the default confidence interval at 0.95 (95 per cent). Click on OK. The analysis as shown in figure 8.5 will appear.

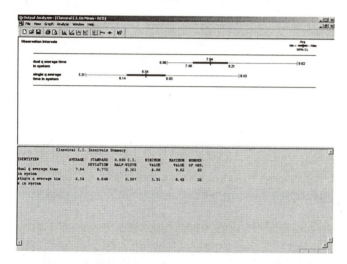

Figure 8.5   ARENA confidence interval on mean analysis (20 replications)

Using the ARENA output processor the results show that we can be 95 per cent confident that the dual queue time in system is between 7.48 and 8.20 minutes and the single queue average time in system is between 6.14 and 6.94 minutes.

In order to assess the effect of an increase in the number of replications the analysis is repeated with 100 replications and the results presented in figure 8.6.

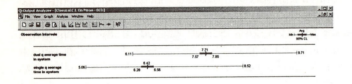

Figure 8.6   ARENA confidence interval on mean analysis (100 replications)

The use of 100 rather than 20 replications has allowed us to produce a more statistically precise estimate of the average queue times. The half-width for dual queue average time in system has been reduced from 0.361 to 0.137 and the half-width for single queue average time in system has been reduced from 0.397 to 0.137. Thus the results show that we can be 95% confident that the dual queue average time in system is between 7.57 and 7.85 minutes and the single queue average time in system between 6.28 and 6.56 minutes.

Confidence Interval Analysis using SIMUL8

SIMUL8 can be used to analyse the bank clerk simulation constructed in chapter 6. Before the analysis can begin however an adjustment to the code must be made to ensure the simulation is a true terminating system. At present the simulation starts from empty and then customers arrive at the bank with a run-time specified of 480 minutes. To be a true terminating system the simulation must reach its starting condition (i.e. empty system) at the end of its run. To achieve this, the simulation must stop receiving new customers after a certain time period and then service any remaining customers in the system. One method of achieving this is to add an additional condition to the SIMUL8 work entry point objects which directs all customers after 'closing time' away from the bank. To update the bank clerk simulation to a terminating system load the single queue bank clerk simulation into SIMUL8 (see chapter 6). Place a new work exit point on the screen and connect the work entry points 1 and 2 to it using the route drawing mode button on the toolbar. Double click on the work entry point 1 object and click on the label actions button. Click on add, then new and type in the name route to take. Ensure the radiobutton is set to number. This creates an attribute (label) which tells the simulation which routing each customer should take through the model. To define the routing logic click on the IF... Visual logic button. Press the 'ins' key to insert a line of code. Select the Set... option from the menu. In the dialog box select the route to take object (the radiobutton should be set on object) and set the calculation box to 1. Press the 'ins' key again and select the IF... option from the menu and the formula editor appears. Select the simulation time object from the list, select the 'is more than' option for equality condition and enter 480 in the calculation box (see figure 8.7).

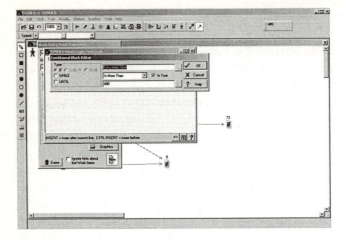

Figure 8.7 Using the conditional block editor

Press the 'ins' key again, select the set option from the menu and select the route to take object (the radiobutton should be set to object). Enter 2 for the calculation amount. The visual logic code should be as in figure 8.8.

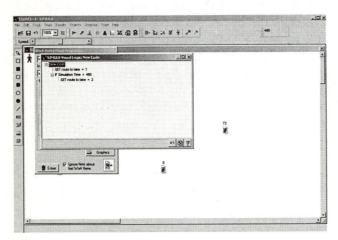

Figure 8.8 Entering the visual logic code

The code thus sets the label 'route to take' to 1 for every customer at this work entry point. If the simulation time is greater than 480 minutes however the 'route to take' label has a value of 2. Click on the routing out button on the work entry object and the screen should appear as in figure 8.9. SIMUL8 has associated a value of 1 with the route to the queue for work centre 1 and a value of 2 for the work complete 2 object. Make sure the radiobutton for the label 'discipline' is checked and press the detail button to check that the label 'route to take' is used to set the label 'value'.

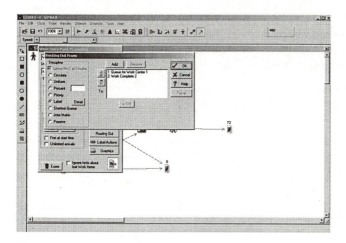

Figure 8.9 Entering the routing out details

Repeat the above for the work entry point 2 object. Thus all customers will travel to the work centre as before, unless the time exceeds 480 minutes when they are directed out of the model to work complete 2 object. The next step is to alter the run-length to 510 minutes (providing 30 minutes to empty the system). Do this by selecting the Trials/Results Collection Period option from the menu and enter 510. Select the Trials/Conduct Trials option from the menu and enter the number of runs as 20. Click on OK and the simulation will run for 20 replications and the results screen will appear (figure 8.10).

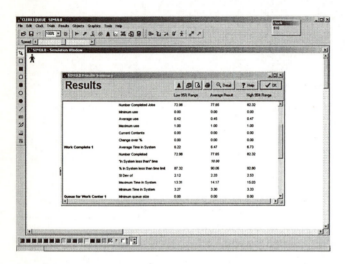

Figure 8.10 SIMUL8 results screen

The results show that we can be 95 per cent confident that the single queue time in system is between 6.22 and 6.73 minutes.

The above procedure is repeated for the dual queue system. Change the resource from 1 bank clerk with a capacity of 2, to 2 bank clerks each with a capacity of 1. The visual logic code is slightly more complex as there needs to be code directing customers to the shortest queue. Again if the simulation time is greater than 480 minutes all customers are directed out of the simulation. The visual logic code for the work entry points 1 and 2 should be as in figure 8.11.

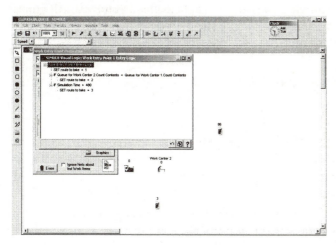

Figure 8.11 Entering the visual logic code

When running the simulation for 20 replications the results show that we can be 95 per cent confident that the single queue time in system is between 6.81 and 7.32 minutes.

In order to assess the effect of an increase in the number of replications the analysis is repeated with 100 replications. The use of 100 rather than 20 replications has allowed us to produce a more statistically precise estimate of the average queue times. The results showed that we can be 95 per cent confident that the dual queue average time in system is between 7.03 and 7.24 minutes and the single queue average time in system between 6.46 and 6.73 minutes.

Establishing Confidence Intervals at a Given Half-Width

There are instances when we wish to specify the half-width of the confidence intervals, thus providing a predetermined measure of precision for the presentation of our results. In general, more replications conducted will lead to a narrower confidence interval, but the actual number to achieve a particular level of precision cannot be calculated in advance as it is a function of the sample size itself. An approximate value can be gained however by obtaining an initial sample standard deviation (say from five to ten replications) and solving for n as follows:

$$n = (z_{1-\alpha/2} * s_o / h_w)^2$$

where
$z_{1-\alpha/2}$ = value from normal distribution table at a significance α
s_o = sample standard deviation
hw = required half-width of confidence interval

Note that $t_{1-\alpha/2, df}$ has been approximated to $z_{1-\alpha/2}$ because df depends on n which is the target value. When n replications have been completed the confidence intervals are calculated in the normal way. If the half-width is greater than required then the current value of s can be used to recalculate the number of replications, n, required.

Establishing Confidence Intervals at a Given Half-Width using EXCEL

Figure 8.12 shows the spreadsheet to calculate the required replications in order to obtain a half-width of 0.2 minutes for server queue time in the booking clerk example. The sample standard deviation is taken from the figure calculated for 20 replications shown in figure 8.1. The EXCEL spreadsheet function NORMSINV is used to provide a z-value at a significance level of 0.05. The results show that approximately 41 and 49 replications are needed to measure the dual queue bank clerk average time in system and single queue bank clerk average time in system respectively in order to meet the target half-width of 0.2 minutes.

	A	B	C	D
30	Required Replication at target half-width of 0.2 minutes			
31				formulae for dual queue
32	Sample Standard Deviation	0.77	0.85	=B23
33	Z value (a=0.05)	-1.64	-1.64	=NORMSINV(0.05)
34	Target half-width	0.20	0.20	1.0
35	Required Replications	40.39	48.49	=POWER(B33*B32/B34,2)

Figure 8.12 Spreadsheet for required replications for target half-width

Establishing Confidence Intervals at a Given Half-Width using ARENA

Normally a fixed number of iterations are made (say ten) without knowing the size of the confidence intervals of the values we are measuring. We can use ARENA to check a particular confidence interval value after each simulation run and automatically stop running when this target value is reached. To do this we need some additional modules to control the simulation run behaviour.

Load in the terminating dual queue bank clerk simulation file (figure 8.4). Add a Create, Decide, Assign and Dispose module to the simulation screen away from the main model. Double click on the create module and enter 1 for max arrivals to create one entity at the beginning of each simulation replication. Double click on the decide module. Select the n-way by condition type. Add the expression NREP <= 2. NREP is an ARENA variable holding the number of replications made. This condition ensures that at least two replications have been made and thus a confidence interval is formed. Add the expression ORUNHALF(1) > 0.2. ORUNHALF(1) is an ARENA variable holding the value of the confidence interval 1 (defined in the number field of the outputs module). This condition runs the simulation until the defined half-width is less than the target value of 0.2. Double click on the assign module. Click on the Add button. Select the other option. Enter MREP for other and NREP for new value. This sets the number of replications (MREP) to the current number of replications executed (NREP) causing the simulation to stop at the end of the current replication. Select the run/setup/replication parameters option from the menu. Enter 99999 for the Number of Replications parameter. This is an arbitrarily high number, the replication number in this case being controlled by the confidence interval coding. Connect the modules using the connect button as in figure 8.13. Run the model.

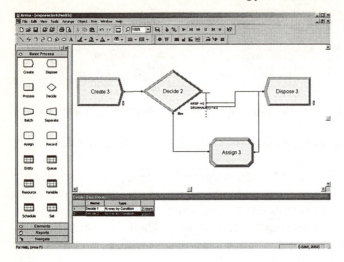

Figure 8.13 Logic for establishing confidence intervals at a given width

The confidence interval for the dual queue average time in system (figure 8.14) is given as 0.198 (below the 0.2) target value. Note the number of replications required to reach this value is 42, which is close to the 49 predicted by the spreadsheet (figure 8.12). Differences in the exact number of replication required are mainly due to the fact that the spreadsheet calculations are based on an estimate of the variance from an initial small sample of only 20 replications.

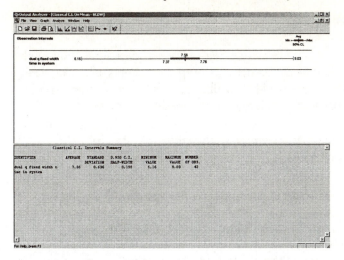

Figure 8.14 ARENA confidence interval for analysis at a given width

Establishing Confidence Intervals at a Given Half-Width using SIMUL8

No automatic way of providing results at a given half-width is given here (you will need to utilise the Visual Logic and Visual Basic facilities of SIMUL8 which are beyond the scope of this book), but you can use the spreadsheet template in figure 8.12 to provide an estimate of the number of replications required. Run the simulation using SIMUL8 and adjust the number of runs as necessary to obtain the necessary half-width observed in the results summary. The half-width can be calculated by taking the maximum value at the 95 per cent level and subtracting the average value.

Comparing Alternatives

When comparing between alternative configurations of a simulation model
we need to test whether differences in output measures are statistically
significant or if differences could be within the bounds of random variation.
Alternative configurations which require this analysis include:

- changing input parameters (e.g. changing arrival rate),
- changing system rules (e.g. changing priority at a decision point),
- changing system configuration (comparing manual versus
  automated system).

Whatever the scale of the differences between alternative configurations
there is a need to undertake statistical tests. The tests will be considered for
comparing between two alternatives and then between more than two
alternatives.

The following assumptions are made when undertaking the tests:

- The data collected *within* a given alternative are independent
  observations of a random variable. This can be obtained by each
  replication using a different set of random numbers (Method of
  Independent Replications).

- The data collected *between* alternatives are independent
  observations of a random variable. This can be obtained by using a
  separate number stream for each alternative. This can be
  implemented by changing the seeds of the random number
  generator between runs (e.g. using the SEEDS command in
  ARENA). Note however that certain tests use the ability to use
  common random numbers for each simulation run in their analysis
  (see paired t-test using common random numbers).

Hypothesis Testing

When comparing simulation scenarios we want to know if the results of the
simulation for each scenario are different because of random variability or
because of an actual change in performance. In statistical terms we can do
this using a hypothesis test to see if the sample means of each scenario
differ.

An hypothesis test makes an assumption or hypothesis (termed the null hypothesis, H_0) and tries to disprove it. Acceptance of the null hypothesis implies that there is insufficient evidence to reject it (it does not prove that it is true). Rejection of the null hypothesis however means that the alternative hypothesis (H_1) is accepted. The null hypothesis is tested using a test statistic (based on an appropriate sampling distribution) at a particular significance level α which relates to the area called the critical region in the tail of the distribution being used. If the test statistic (which we calculate), lies in the critical region, the result is unlikely to have occurred by chance and so the null hypothesis would be rejected. The boundaries of the critical region, called the critical values, depend on whether the test is two-tailed (we have no reason to believe that a rejection of the null hypothesis implies that the test statistic is either greater or less than some assumed value) or one-tailed (we have reason to believe that a rejection of the null hypothesis implies that the test statistic is either greater or less than some assumed value).

We must also consider the fact that the decision to reject or not reject the null hypothesis is based on a probability. Thus at a 5 per cent significance level there is a 5 per cent chance that H_0 will be rejected when it is in fact true. In statistical terminology this is called a type I error. The converse of this is accepting the null hypothesis when it is in fact false, called a type II error. Usually α values of 0.05 (5%) or 0.01 (1%) are used. An alternative to testing at a particular significance level is to calculate the p-value which is the lowest level of significance at which the observed value of the test statistic is significant. Thus a p-value of 0.045 (indicating a type I error occurring 45 times out of 1000) would show that the null hypothesis would be rejected at 0.05, but only by a small amount.

Comparison between the Bank Clerk Models

To demonstrate the use of statistical tests for comparing between different types of models, a comparison will be made between the single queue and dual queue bank clerk models developed in chapter 6. In chapter 6 the results from the single queue bank clerk system and the dual queue bank clerk system were compared. There are two potential problems with using these results for decision-making. The first problem is that these results are from a single run of the model. Each time the model is run a different result will occur due to the random numbers in arrival and service times. This problem has been tackled in this chapter by the use of independent replications to generate a confidence interval around the mean. The second problem is judging whether the two means (over the replications) do actually suggest that a statistical change in performance has taken place. For instance if the mean for the single queue scenario is 4.8 minutes and the mean for the dual queue scenario is 5.1 minutes, do these measures represent a statistically significant difference in performance or are they within the boundary of random variation? One quick way of making this judgement is to compare the confidence intervals for the two means (figure 8.5) and if they do not overlap we can say the difference between the means is statistically significant. This is an informal test however and in order to quantify how sure we are of this difference we need to conduct an hypothesis test which will provide us with a decision based on a chosen level of confidence (e.g. 95 per cent or 99 per cent).

The two-sample t-test provides a comparison between two systems. The test requires the independence assumption and there is also an assumption that the data being measured is normally distributed (see 'testing for normality' section to check if the data is normally distributed). Generally the paired t-test is used to compare alternatives of real systems.

Paired t-test

The test calculates the difference between the two alternatives for each replication. It tests the hypothesis that if the data from both models is from the same distribution then the mean of the differences will be zero. The test contains the following steps:

1. Formulate the null hypothesis.
Null Hypothesis: The means of both data sets are equal.
Alternative Hypothesis: The means of both data sets are different.

2. Set a significance level.
A significance level of $\alpha = 0.05$ is usual.

3. Compute the t value.

$$t = \frac{\overline{x}_d - \mu_d}{\sigma_{\overline{d}}}$$

$\overline{x}_d$ = sample mean of the n differences
μ_d = population mean difference if the null hypothesis is correct
$\sigma_{\overline{d}}$ = standard error of the mean difference

where

$$\sigma_{\bar{d}} = \frac{s_d}{\sqrt{n}}$$

where
s_d = standard deviation of the difference s
n = number of differences

4. Interpret the results.

The critical value is then found from a t table for α significance level and n-1 degrees of freedom. If calculated t value > lookup value then the hypothesis that the mean differences are zero is rejected.

The test will now be undertaken using the EXCEL and ARENA software.

Undertaking a Paired t-test using EXCEL

Excel can be used to undertake the paired t-test if the data for each replication is entered on to the spreadsheet. Figure 8.16 shows the average time in system recorded for each replication of the simulation for the two experiments in cells B3:C22. The spreadsheet functions average, minimum and maximum are used to calculate these values for each experiment in cells B24 to C26. The paired t-test is undertaken using the EXCEL Data Analysis toolkit by selecting the Tools/Data Analysis... option. Select the t-test: Paired Two-Sample for Means option from the menu. The dialog box in figure 8.15 will appear. Enter the variable 1 range as the data range covering experiment 1. Enter the variable 2 range as the data range covering experiment 2.

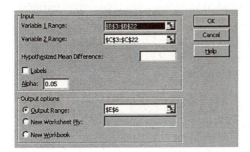

Figure 8.15 EXCEL paired t-test dialog box

Enter a cell value for the top left-hand of the EXCEL generated output. EXCEL will generate the analysis shown in figure 8.16 in cells E6 to G19.

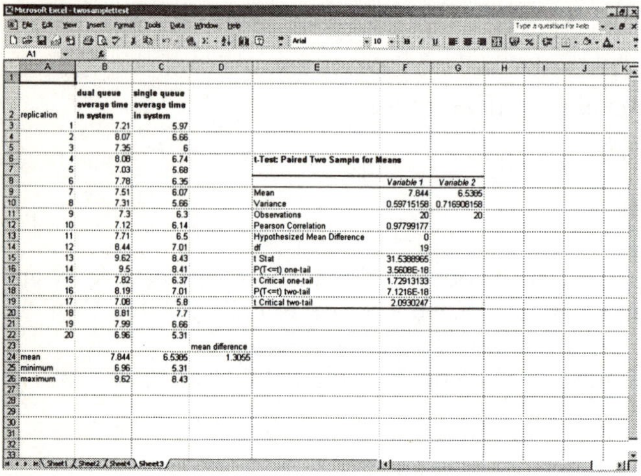

Microsoft Excel - twosampletttest

replication	dual queue average time in system	single queue average time in system
1	7.21	5.97
2	8.07	6.66
3	7.35	6
4	8.08	6.74
5	7.03	5.68
6	7.78	6.35
7	7.51	6.07
8	7.31	5.66
9	7.3	6.3
10	7.12	6.14
11	7.71	6.5
12	8.44	7.01
13	9.62	8.43
14	9.5	8.41
15	7.82	6.37
16	8.19	7.01
17	7.08	5.8
18	8.81	7.7
19	7.99	6.66
20	6.96	5.31
mean	7.844	6.5385
minimum	6.96	5.31
maximum	9.62	8.43

mean difference 1.3055

t-Test: Paired Two Sample for Means

	Variable 1	Variable 2
Mean	7.844	6.5385
Variance	0.59715158	0.716908158
Observations	20	20
Pearson Correlation	0.97799177	
Hypothesized Mean Difference	0	
df	19	
t Stat	31.5388965	
P(T<=t) one-tail	3.5608E-18	
t Critical one-tail	1.72913133	
P(T<=t) two-tail	7.1216E-18	
t Critical two-tail	2.0930247	

Figure 8.16 Paired t-test using EXCEL

The t stat value of 31.5 is greater than the t critical value (two-tail) of 2.09 so we reject the null hypothesis and accept there is a difference in the average time in system for each experiment.

Undertaking a Paired t-test using ARENA

In order to demonstrate the use of the paired t-test a comparison will be made between two versions of the bank clerk simulation. The single queue version of the model will be compared to the model with the dual queue operation. The test will attempt to discover if this change has a measurable effect on the performance of the simulation, over and above any variation caused by the randomness of the models. If a statistically significant change is detected then the test will provide an estimate of the amount of change in model performance caused by the change in arrival rate.

1. State the hypothesis.
Null Hypothesis: The means of both data sets are equal.
Alternative Hypothesis: The means of both data sets are different.

2. A significance level of 0.05 will be used.

3. Compute the test statistic.

Experiment 1- Dual Queue Load in the terminating dual queue bank clerk model. Select the run/setup/replication option from the menu. Enter 20 for the 'Number of Replications' parameter. Run the bank clerk model. This will create the data file BCD.DAT which provides information on the customer time in system for each replication.

Experiment 2- Single Queue Load in the single queue terminating bank clerk model. Select the run/setup/replication option from the menu. Enter 20 for the 'Number of Replications' parameter. Run the model. This will create the data file BCS.DAT.

Undertake the paired t-test analysis by running the output analyzer program. Select the Analyze/Compare Means option from the menu. Select the Add File option and enter BCD.DAT for Data File A. Set replications to Lumped. Enter BCS.DAT for Data File B. Set replications to Lumped. Select OK. Select the 'Paired t-test' radiobutton. Select OK. The ARENA analysis is shown in figure 8.17.

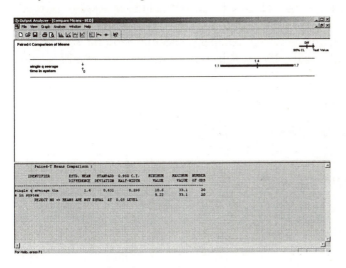

Figure 8.17 Paired t-test using ARENA

4. Interpret the results.

The results in figure 8.17 show that the null hypothesis is rejected, so the means are different (with a mean difference of 1.4 minutes) at a 0.05

significance level. Thus the change in average time in system is statistically significant between the single queue and dual queue bank clerk models.

Undertaking a Paired t-test using SIMUL8

You can undertake this test by exporting the simulation results to a spreadsheet and conducting the analysis shown in figure 8.16. To export the simulation results create a new spreadsheet file in EXCEL.

The quickest way to export the time in system measure is by running the model and clicking on the work complete 1 icon and selecting the results button. Click on the histogram icon and a graph will be displayed in a new window. Right click on the graph and select the copy data option from the pull-down menu. Go to EXCEL and place the cursor on the cell where the data should appear and right click. Select the paste option on the pull-down menu and the simulation time and time in system measures will be displayed in the spreadsheet.

To export any performance measure select the Results/Results Export option and click the tick box labelled 'Include in Results Export'. Click on the browse button and locate the new spreadsheet file you have created. Enter a sheet name which matches a sheet name in the spreadsheet such as sheet1. Tick on the Every Run box in the exports results section (see figure 8.18).

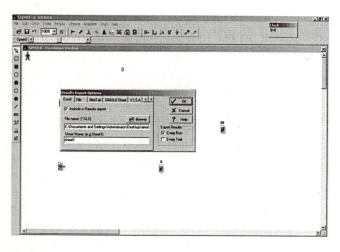

Figure 8.18 Exporting results to a spreadsheet file

To export only selected data items such as the time in system measure, select the Results/Results Summary option from the main menu. Click on the detail button and then click on the 'All Results Off' button. Then click on the object you wish to be reported from the object list. In this case the 'work complete 1' object. Click on the 'Results' button to report on this variable. Run the simulation and only the results for the items selected will be displayed and exported to the spreadsheet.

Paired t-test using Common Random Numbers

The idea of using common random numbers (CRN) is to ensure that alternative configurations of a model differ only due to those configurations and not due to the different random number sets used to drive the random variables within the model. It is important that synchronisation of random variables occurs across the model configurations, so the use of a dedicated random number stream for each random variate is recommended. Again as with other variance reduction techniques the success of the method will be dependent on the model structure and there is no certainty that variance will be actually reduced. Another important point is that by driving the alternative model configuration with the same random numbers we are assuming that they will behave in a similar manner to large or small values of the random variables driving the models. In general it is advisable to conduct a pilot study to ensure that the CRN technique is in fact reducing the variance between alternatives.

Because the output from a simulation model is a random variable the variance of that output will determine the precision of the results obtained from it. Statistical techniques to reduce that variance may be used to either obtain smaller confidence intervals for a fixed amount of simulating time or achieve a desired confidence interval with a smaller amount of simulating.

A variety of variance reduction techniques (VRT) are discussed in Law and Kelton (2000). The use of common random numbers (CRN) in conjunction with the paired t-test is described for comparing alternative system configurations. The paired t-test approach assumes the data is normally distributed (see 'testing for normality' section to check if the data is normally distributed) but does not assume all observations from the two alternatives are independent of each other, as does the two-sample-t approach.

The next section shows an example of using a paired t-test with common random numbers using the ARENA software.

Undertaking a Paired t-test with Common Random Numbers using ARENA

1. State the hypothesis.

Null Hypothesis: The means of both data sets are equal.
Alternative Hypothesis: The means of both data sets are different.

2. A significance level of 0.05 will be used.

3. Compute the test statistic.

Load in the terminating dual queue bank clerk model. In this experiment common random numbers will be used in each simulation scenario. In this case the interarrival times and the process times will require synchronisation. To undertake an analysis using common random numbers in ARENA place a SEEDS module on the model window from the elements template. Double click on the SEEDS module, click on Add and enter the arrive1 identifier. Select common for the initialize option. Repeat this process for arrive2, process1 and process2 parameters. Select the arrive1 module. Change the time between parameter from EXPO(10) to EXPO(10,arrive1) to assign the random number stream. Click on the assign button and change the process time parameter UNIFORM(2,6) to UNIFORM(2,6,process1). Repeat the above for the arrive2 module. In the outputs module change the BCD.DAT file name to BCDS.DAT. Run the bank clerk model in its original form for 20 replications. This will create the data file BCDS.DAT. Repeat the above for the single queue bank clerk model. In the outputs module change the BCS.DAT file name to BCSS.DAT. Run the model for 20 replications. This will create the data file BCSS.DAT. Undertake the paired t-test analysis by running the output analyzer and selecting the Analyze/Compare Means option from the menu. Select the Add File option. Enter BCDS.DAT for Data File A. Set replications to Lumped. Enter BCSS.DAT for Data File B. Set replications to Lumped. Select OK. Select the 'paired t-test' radiobutton. Select OK. The ARENA analysis is shown in figure 8.19.

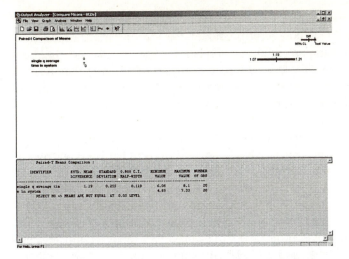

Figure 8.19 Paired t-test using ARENA with CRN

4. Interpret the results.

The results in figure 8.19 show that the null hypothesis is rejected, so the alternative hypothesis is accepted, so the means are different at a 0.05 significance level. Thus the change in arrival rate for type 2 customers does have a statistically significant effect on the bank clerk queue times. Note the narrower half-width value for the paired t-test with CRN of 0.119 compared to the paired t-test of 0.295.

One-Way ANOVA

One-way analysis of variance (ANOVA) is used to compare the means of several alternative systems. Several replications are performed of each alternative and the test attempts to determine whether the variation in output performance is due to differences *between* the alternatives or due to inherent randomness *within* the alternatives themselves. This is undertaken by comparing the ratio of the two variations with a test statistic. The test makes the following assumptions:

- Independent data both within and between the data sets.
- Observations from each alternative are drawn from a normal distribution.
- The normal distributions have the same variance.

The first assumption implies the collection of data using independent runs or the batch means technique, but precludes the use of variance reduction techniques (e.g. common random numbers). The second assumption implies that each output measure is the mean of a large number of observations. This assumption is usually valid but can be tested with the chi-square or Kolmogorov-Smirnov test if required. The third assumption may require an increase in replication run-length to decrease the variances of mean performance. The F-test can be used to test this assumption if required. The test finds if a significant difference between means is apparent but does not indicate if all the means are different, or if the difference is between particular means. To identify where the differences occur then tests such as Tukeys HSD test may be used (Black, 1994). Alternatively confidence intervals between each combination can provide an indication (Law and Kelton, 2000). The ANOVA analysis will now be undertaken using EXCEL and ARENA software.

Undertaking the ANOVA Analysis using EXCEL

EXCEL can be used to undertake the ANOVA analysis if the data for each replication is entered on to the spreadsheet. Figure 8.21 shows the single queue bank clerk simulation recorded for each replication of the simulation for the three experiments (an interarrival rate for customer type 2 of 10, 12 and 14 minutes) in cells B3:C52. The spreadsheet functions average, minimum and maximum are used to calculate these values for each experiment in cells B24 to D26. The ANOVA is undertaken using the EXCEL Data Analysis toolkit. Select the Tools/Data Analysis option. Select the Anova: Single Factor option from the menu. The dialog box in figure 8.20 will appear. Enter the variable range as the data range covering all three experiments. Enter the output range as a cell value for the top left-hand of the EXCEL generated output.

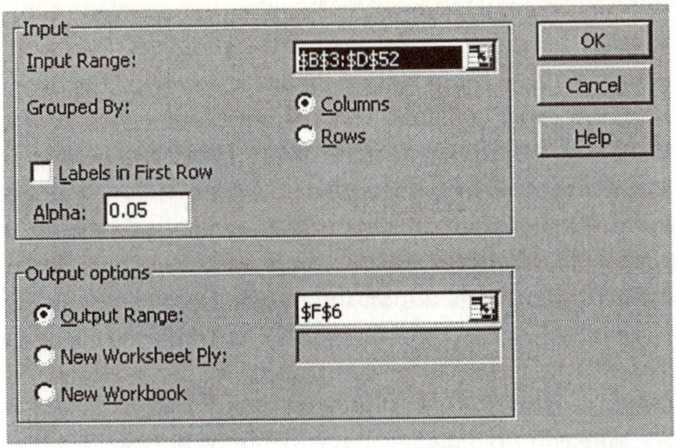

Figure 8.20 EXCEL Anova: Single Factor dialog box

EXCEL will generate the analysis shown in figure 8.21 in cells F6 to L20.

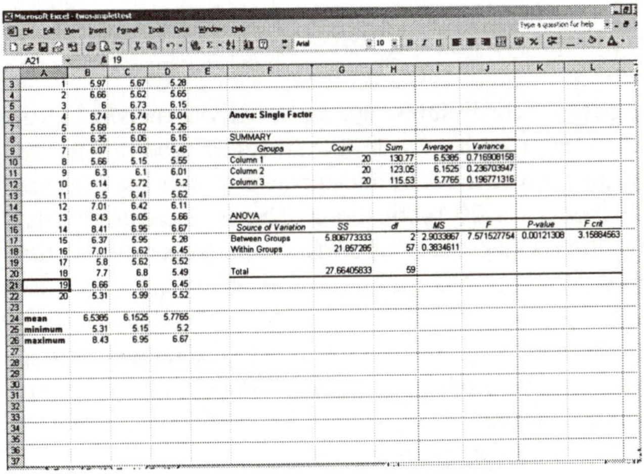

Figure 8.21 ANOVA analysis using EXCEL

The F-test value of 7.57 is greater than the F critical value of 3.16 (alternatively the p value of 0.0012 is less than the significance level of 0.05) so we reject the null hypothesis and accept that there is a difference in the customer time in system for each experiment. Further analysis is required to locate where the difference lies.

Undertaking a One-Way ANOVA Test using ARENA

In order to demonstrate the use of the ANOVA test a comparison will be made between three versions of the bank clerk simulation. The model results will be compared with an arrival rate for type 2 customers which will be set with an exponential distribution with a mean of 10, 12 and 14 minutes. The test will attempt to discover if these changes have a measurable effect on the performance of the simulation, over and above any variation caused by the randomness within the model parameters.

1. State the hypothesis.
Null Hypothesis: All data sets have the same mean.
Alternative Hypothesis: At least two data sets have different means.

2. A significance level of 0.05 will be used.

3. Compute the test statistic.

Load in the terminating single queue bank clerk simulation.

Experiment 1 Double click on the outputs module. Click on the edit button. Enter the filename "ANOVA1.DAT" (with quotes) for the output file. Set the arrival rate for customer type 1 to 15 and the arrival rate for customer type 2 to 10. Run the model for 20 replications. This will create the data files ANOVA1.DAT which will provide information on the customer time in system for each replication.

Experiment 2 Set the customer type 2 arrival rate to 12. The data file names require changing to prevent the model overwriting the previous data files. In the outputs module change the ANOVA1.DAT file name to ANOVA2.DAT. Run the model for 20 replications.

Experiment 3 Set the customer type 2 arrival rate to 14. The data file names require changing to prevent the model overwriting the previous data files. In the statistics module change the ANOVA2.DAT file name to ANOVA3.DAT. Run the model for 20 replications.

Undertake the ANOVA analysis by running the output analyzer and selecting the Analyze/One-Way ANOVA option from the menu. Select the Add File option. Enter ANOVA1.DAT for the Data File. Set replications to Lumped. Select the Add File option. Enter ANOVA2.DAT for the Data

File. Set replications to Lumped. Select the Add File option. Enter ANOVA3.DAT for the Data File. Set replications to Lumped. Select Comparison Method to Tukey. The ANOVA entry screen is shown in figure 8.22.

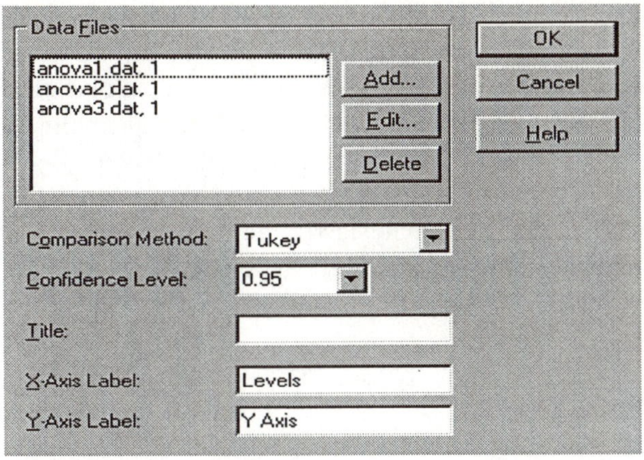

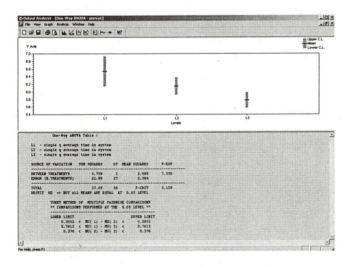

Figure 8.22 ARENA entry screen for ANOVA analysis

The ARENA analysis is shown in figure 8.23.

Figure 8.23 ARENA one-way ANOVA analysis

4. Interpret the results.

From the results screen it can be seen that the null hypothesis has been rejected (the F-test statistic of 7.55 is greater than the critical value of 3.159) and so the alternative hypothesis is accepted, so the means are different at a 0.05 significance level. What the basic ANOVA analysis does not tell us is which means are different. In this case a comparison between the means has been made using the Tukey HSD (honestly significant differences) method. ARENA also provides other methods of multiple comparisons. The Tukey method provides a comparison test between all the pairs of means in the analysis. In this case there are three comparisons (1->2, 1->3 and 2->3) to be made. The analysis (figure 8.23) computes a difference between all the pairs of means which are as follows:

1->2   0.3855
1->3   0.7615
2->3   0.3760

These differences are then compared to a critical range, which when the sample sizes are equal, uses the following formula:

$$Critical\ \ Range\ = Q_{(c,n-c)}\sqrt{\frac{MSE}{n}}$$

where
MSE = Mean Square Error within groups
n = sample size
$Q_{(c,n-c)}$ = critical value of the student Q statistic
where
c = pairs of means
(n − c) = degrees of freedom

thus

$$Critical\ \ Range\ = Q_{(3,60-3)}\sqrt{\frac{0.384}{20}}$$

from cutoff values of selected studentized range distributions table $Q_{(3,57)}$ = 3.4

therefore Critical Range = 3.4 * 0.139 = 0.4726

Comparing the differences between pairs of means for the comparison 1 -> 2 has a difference (0.3855) below the critical range of 0.4726. Thus there is no significant difference between the means of pairs 1 and 2. The difference between pairs of means for the comparison 1 -> 3 has a difference (0.7615) above the critical range of 0.4726. Thus there is a significant difference between the means of pairs 1 and 3. The difference between the pairs of means for comparison 2 -> 3 has a difference (0.3760) below the critical range of 0.4726. Thus there is no significant difference between the means of pairs 2 and 3.

Undertaking a One-Way ANOVA Test using SIMUL8

You can undertake this test by exporting the simulation results to a spreadsheet and conducting the analysis shown in figure 8.21.

Factorial Designs

So far analysis of simulation experimentation has focused on determining the statistical significance of a change in an input variable. The experimentation may however wish to analyse the effect of making changes to a variety of inputs and/or making a number of changes to a particular variable and to see the effect on a number of output variables. In experimental design terminology experiments are conducted by changing a factor (input variable) in the model which has a level (value). A particular combination of levels is called a treatment. The output variable of interest is called the response. The standard way to investigate changes in a level of a factor would be to make a simulation run for each level and record the response. There are two problems with this approach:

- to investigate a number of factors requires a relatively high number of simulation runs,
- the effects of interaction (i.e. whether the effect of one factor depends on the levels of the other).

Thus the objective of factorial design is to determine the impact of factors on a response.

Two-Level Full-Factorial Design

A two-level full-factorial design is when each factor is set at just two (high and low) levels. The levels could be different values of an input variable or different configurations of a model (e.g. different scheduling rules for a queuing system). No rules are provided as to what the levels of the factors should be, but levels need to be set that are different enough to show how the factor affects response, but within normal operating conditions for that factor. For a full-factorial design each possible combination of factor levels is tested for response. This means for k factors there are 2^k combinations of low and high factor levels. These possible combinations are shown in an array called the design matrix. A design matrix for a 2^3 factorial design (i.e. three factors) is shown in table 8.1.

Table 8.1 2^3 factorial design matrix

Factor Combination	Factor 1	Factor 2	Factor 3	Response
1	-	-	-	R_1
2	+	-	-	R_2
3	-	+	-	R_3
4	+	+	-	R_4
5	-	-	+	R_5
6	+	-	+	R_6
7	-	+	+	R_7
8	+	+	+	R_8

The advantage of following the factorial design approach over varying a single factor at a time, is that the effect of interaction effects can be assessed. The ability to assess the impact of one factor change when the level of a second factor changes is important in finding the best system performance because the effect of two factors changing may not be the same as the addition of the effect of each factor change in isolation. For more on factorial design experiments see Law and Kelton (2000).

Statistical Analysis for Non-Terminating Systems

The previous section considered statistical analysis for terminating systems. This section provides details of techniques for analysing steady-state systems in which the start conditions of the model are not returned to. These techniques involve more complex analysis than for a terminating system and so consideration should be given to treating the model as a terminating system if at all possible.

A non-terminating system generally goes through an initial transient phase and then enters a steady-state phase when its condition is independent of the simulation starting conditions. This behaviour could relate to a manufacturing system starting from an empty ('no-inventory') state and then after a period of time moving to a stabilised behaviour pattern. A simulation analysis will be directed towards measuring performance during the steady-state phase and avoiding measurements during the initial transient phase. The following methods of achieving this are discussed:

Setting Starting Conditions

This approach involves specifying start conditions for the simulation which will provide a quick transition to steady-state conditions. Most simulations are started in an empty state for convenience but by using knowledge of steady-state conditions (e.g. stock levels) it is possible to reduce the initial bias phase substantially. The disadvantage with this approach is the effort in initialising simulation variables, of which there may be many, and when a suitable initial value may not be known. Also it is unlikely that the initial transient phase will be eliminated entirely. For these reasons the warm up period method is often used.

Using a Warm Up Period

Instead of manually entering starting conditions this approach uses the model to initialise the system and thus provide starting conditions automatically. This approach discards all measurements collected on a performance variable before a preset time in order to ensure that no data is collected during the initial phase. The point at which data is discarded must be set late enough to ensure that the simulation has entered the steady-state phase, but not so late that insufficient data points can be collected for a reasonably precise statistical analysis. A popular method of choosing the discard point is to visually inspect the simulation output behaviour of the variable over time. Welch (1983) suggests a procedure using the moving average value in order to smooth the output response (i.e. separate the long-term trend values from short-term fluctuations). It is important to ensure that the model is inspected over a time period which allows infrequent events (e.g. machine breakdown) to occur a reasonable number of times.

In order to determine the behaviour of the system over time and in particular to identify steady-state behaviour, a performance measure must be chosen. A value such as work-in-progress (WIP) provides a useful measure of overall system behaviour. In a manufacturing setting this could relate to the amount of material within the system at any one time. In a service setting (as is the case with the bank clerk model) the work-in-progress measure represents the number of customers in the system. While this measure will vary over time in a steady-state system the long-term level of WIP should remain constant.

Using an Extended Run-Length

This approach simply consists of running the simulation for an extended run-length, so reducing the bias introduced on output variables in the initial transient phase. This approach is best applied in combination with one or both of the previous approaches.

Batch Means Analysis

To avoid repeatedly discarding data during the initial transient phase for each run, an alternative approach allows all data to be collected during one long run. The batch means method consists of making one very long run of the simulation and collecting data at intervals during the run. Each interval between data collection is termed a batch. Each batch is treated as a separate run of the simulation for analysis. The batch means method is suited to systems that have very long warm up periods and so avoidance of multiple replications is desirable. However with the increase in computing power available this advantage has diminished, with run-lengths needing to be extremely long in order to slow down analysis considerably. The batch means method also requires the use of statistical analysis methods which are beyond the scope of this book (see Law and Kelton, 2000).

Statistical Analysis of the Non-Terminating Bank Clerk Simulation

Statistical analysis for non-terminating systems will now be undertaken using the bank clerk simulation model with the ARENA and SIMUL8 software.

Statistical Analysis of the Non-Terminating Bank Clerk Simulation using ARENA

Load the terminating version of the single queue bank clerk simulation in ARENA. Select run/setup/project parameters from the menu bar. Enter 20 for the 'Number of Replications' parameter and enter 10000 for the replication length. Ensure the tick boxes (in the 'Initialise between replications' area) are checked for 'System' and 'Statistics' to achieve statistically independent replications.

In order to save information to a data file for analysis we use the statistics module from the advanced process template. To use the advanced process template click on the template attach icon on the toolbar and select the advanced process template file. Click on the STATISTICS module and drag on to the simulation window. Click on the module to obtain the spreadsheet view. The statistics module allows statistics to be saved to a data file which can be analysed by the ARENA Output Analyzer. The output analyzer is a program which is supplied with the ARENA system (it may need to be installed and run separately from the main ARENA system). Enter tis in the name field of the statistics module, select time-persistent from the type menu, enter timeinsys for expression, enter tis for report label and tis.dat for the output file. This will write all values of the variable timeinsys to the external file tis.dat data file.

To collect statistics on the average time in system double click on the assign module which follows the customer type 1 arrival module. Click on the Add button and select attribute for the type field, timein for the attribute name and TNOW for the new value. This assigns the current simulation time (TNOW) to an attribute of that customer named timein. Repeat the procedure for the assign block following the customer type 2 arrival module. Delete the connector between the process and dispose blocks by clicking on the connector line and pressing the Del key on the keyboard. Add an assign block from the Basic Process template by dragging on to the simulation window. Position the assign block between the process and dispose blocks. Click on the connector icon on the toolbar and connect the assign process exit to the assign block and the assign to the process block. Double click on the assign block and select variable for the type field, timeinsys for the variable name and TNOW-timein for the new value. This sets the variable timeinsys to the current time – the time of entry for the customer exiting the system. Thus all the time in system values for each customer are recorded in the variable timeinsys.

Select the fastforward button to run the model for 20 replications and run the output analyzer. Click on the PLOT button and add the filename tis.dat. Choose the replication all option. Click on OK. The plot will be displayed as in figure 8.24.

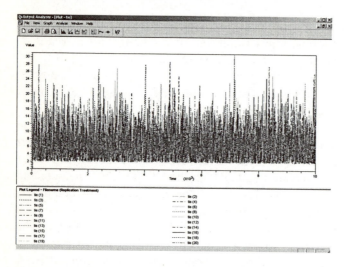

Figure 8.24 Plot of customers in system (10000 minutes)

From figure 8.24 it is clear that a steady-state behaviour is established very quickly. This is not surprising for a simple system with only a single queuing point for customers. The output analyser plot facility can show output for a specified time frame only. Figure 8.25 shows the output for time 0 to 200 minutes.

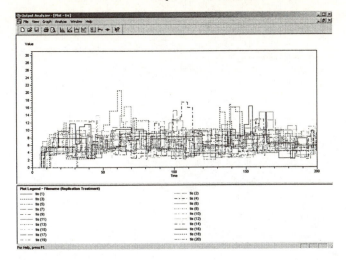

Figure 8.25 Plot of customers in system (first 200 minutes)

From the above plot a warm up period of 50 minutes would seem sufficient. Once a warm up period has been selected the value can be entered in the Run/setup/project parameters dialog box. When entered, the model, when run, will simply discard statistical data during the first 50 minutes of each replication. The model can then be analysed in the same way as a terminating model simulation as outlined earlier in this chapter. Note that when comparing the results of different models the warm up period and run-length will need to be estimated separately for each alternative. Figure 8.26 shows a confidence interval on mean analysis for the non-terminating bank clerk simulation. The analysis should be treated the same as for the terminating analysis but now the analysis is for the steady-state expected performance measures rather than for measures defined in relation to specific starting and ending conditions.

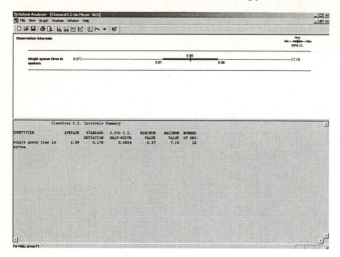

Figure 8.26 Confidence interval on means analysis for non-terminating bank clerk simulation

Using the analysis shows that we can be 95 per cent confident that the average service time for the single queue bank clerk model is between 6.81 and 6.96 minutes with a mean of 6.89 minutes. Note these values are higher than the terminating simulation analysis when the average queue time is 6.54 minutes for 20 replications. This would be expected, as in the steady-state (non-terminating) analysis the system does not empty of customers at the end of each replication and so average queue size will be slightly higher. The confidence interval can be shortened as with the terminating analysis by increasing the number of replications and thus the statistical sample size from which the confidence interval is derived. An alternative way of shortening the confidence interval for steady–state analysis is to increase the run-length for each replication which has the effect of decreasing the variability of each within-run average.

Statistical Analysis of the Non-Terminating Bank Clerk Simulation using SIMUL8

Load in the terminating single queue bank clerk simulation model. Run the model for 10000 minutes and click on the work complete 1 icon and select the results button. Click on the histogram icon and a graph will be displayed in a new window. Right click on the graph and select the copy data option from the pull-down menu. Go to EXCEL and place the cursor on the cell where the data should appear and right click. Select the paste option on the pull-down menu and the simulation time and time in system measures will be displayed in the spreadsheet. Figure 8.27 shows an EXCEL XY graph of the timeinsys values for the single queue model.

An alternative approach to collecting the information is described to demonstrate the use of SIMUL8 labels (attributes) and global data items including data sheets. Select the objects/information store option from the menu. Click the new button and enter the name timeinsys. Select the type spreadsheet. This creates an internal spreadsheet which enables us to save the time in system values for each customer. Click on the new button again and type in countin and select type as number. Set the on reset value as 1. This sets a global data item which we will increment every time a customer enters the simulation and is used to give each data collection value a unique spreadsheet row value. Double click on the work entry 1 object. Select Label Actions and click on the add button. Click on the new button and type in numbin for the label properties. Select the number type. Add the label entrytime in the same way. On the label actions menu click on the numbin label in the list and select the set to radiobutton. Click on the value button and set the distribution to fixed, with a fixed value of countin. Repeat the process for the entrytime variable, setting this to SIMUL8 variable Simulation Time. In the label actions menu, click on the IF Visual logic button. Press the ins key and select the SET option on the menu. Set the information box value to countin and the calculation box to countin=countin+1. Set the numbin, entrytime and countin variables in the work entry point 2 object as before. Double click on the work complete 1 object. Select Label Actions and click on the IF Visual logic button. Press the ins key and select the SET option on the menu. Set the information box value to timeinsys[1,numbin] and the calculation box to Simulation Time. Press the ins key again and select the SET option. Set the information box value to timeinsys[2,numbin] = Simulation Time − entrytime. Repeat the above process for the work complete 2 object. This code saves the current simulation time and the time in system for each customer as they leave the work complete points and leave the system. The times are saved in the first two columns of the SIMUL8 internal spreadsheet which can be pasted to a spreadsheet such as EXCEL.

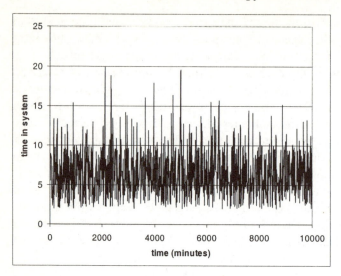

Figure 8.27 Plot of customers in system for 10000 minutes

As in the ARENA example it is clear that a steady-state behaviour is established very quickly (although you would need to graph over multiple replications). This is not surprising for a simple system with only a single queuing point for customers. A warm up period of 50 minutes will be chosen as for the ARENA example earlier. To run the model with a warm up period of 50 minutes select the clock/warm-up period option from the menu and enter 50. When entered, the model, when run, will simply discard statistical data during the first 50 minutes of each replication. Select the clock/results collection period option and enter 9950 to collect results for the next 9950 minutes and so give a total simulation run time of 10000 minutes. Select the trials/conduct trials menu option, enter 20 for the number of runs in trial. Click on OK to run the experiment.

From the results screen the work complete 1 analysis shows that we can be 95 per cent confident that the average service time for the single queue bank clerk model is between 6.78 and 6.90 minutes with a mean of 6.84 minutes. Note these values are higher then the terminating simulation analysis where the average queue time is 6.47 minutes for 20 replications. This would be expected as in the steady-state (non-terminating) analysis the system does not empty of customers at the end of each replication and so average queue size will be slightly higher. The confidence interval can be shortened as with the terminating analysis by increasing the number of replications and thus the statistical sample size from which the confidence interval is derived. An alternative way of shortening the confidence interval for steady-state analysis is to increase the run-length for each replication which has the effect of decreasing the variability of each within-run average.

Summary

Statistical methods are described for analysing terminating and non-terminating systems. For terminating systems, performance measures can be expressed using confidence intervals which include to a certain level of confidence the true mean value of the variable we are measuring. To determine if statistically significant differences are apparent between two different model scenarios the paired t-test may be used. For comparison between several alternatives the one-way ANOVA may be used. If multiple changes are made to a model then the overall impact may differ from the effect of each change in isolation. The use of factorial designs can be used to investigate this behaviour. For non-terminating systems, a steady-state behaviour must be established and identified before the statistical methods for terminating systems can be applied. Steady-state behaviour can be established by setting starting conditions, using a warm up period, using an extended run-length or a combination of the three. Steady-state conditions can be measured using the batch means analysis if a long warm up period makes the method of independent replications infeasible.

Exercises

8.1. Two types of customer arrive at an airport with an exponential interarrival time distribution of five minutes. The first type of customer (accounting for 80 per cent of total customers) proceeds to the check-in desk, goes through customs and X-ray and proceeds to the gate. The second type of customer (accounting for 20 per cent of customers) goes to the ticket counter to purchase tickets and then proceeds as type 1 customers. The process times for ticket buying are exponential with a mean of five minutes. The time for check-in is triangular with parameters of two, four and five minutes. The time for customs and X-ray is exponentially distributed with a mean of one minute. Run the model for 2400 minutes and collect statistics on resource utilisation at each process, queue sizes and time in system for each customer type. Present and interpret the results of the simulation.

8.2. Change the scenario described in exercise 1 so that the check-in and ticket buying desks are combined (with two staff). Compare the results of this model over ten replications with the original using appropriate statistical techniques. Present and interpret the results of the simulation.

8.3. Compare the university car park system described in exercise 6.2 with a system that allows both staff and students to use either car park. Is there a statistically significant difference in the length of time either car park is full in both scenarios? Present and interpret the results of the simulation.

Chapter 9

Implementation

Introduction

This chapter discusses the issue of ensuring that the implementation of change takes place as a result of simulation study results. The need for a detailed project report is outlined in addition to a discussion of managerial and operational involvement in implementation.

Project Report

For each simulation study the simulation model should be accompanied by a project report, outlining the project objectives and providing the results of experimentation. Discussion of results and recommendations for action should also be included. Finally a further work section will communicate to the client any possible developments and subsequent results it is felt could be obtained from the model. If there are a number of results to report, an appendix can be used to document detailed statistical work for example. This enables the main report to focus on the key business results derived from the simulation analysis. A separate technical document may also be prepared which may incorporate a model and/or model details such as key variables and a documented coding listing. Screen shots of the model display can also be used to show model features. If the client is expected to need to develop the code in-house then a detailed explanation of model coding line-by-line will be required. The report structure should contain the following elements:

- Introduction
- Description of the Problem Area
- Model Specification
- Simulation Experimentation
- Results
- Conclusions and Recommendations
- Further Studies
- Appendices: Process Logic, Data Files, Model Coding.

Project Presentation

A good way of 'closing' a simulation project is to organise a meeting of interested parties and present a summary of the project objectives and results. Project documentation can also be distributed at this point. This enables discussion of the outcomes of the project with the client and provides an opportunity to discuss further analysis. This could be in the form of further developments of the current model ('updates' or 'new phase') or a decision to prepare a specification for a new project.

Project Implementation Plan

It is useful to both the simulation developer and client if an implementation plan is formed to undertake recommendations from the simulation study. Implementation issues will usually be handled by the client, but the simulation developer may be needed to provide further interpretation of results or conduct further experimentation. Changes in the system studied may also necessitate model modification. The level of support at this time from the developer may range from a telephone 'hotline' to further personal involvement specified in the project report. Results from a simulation project will only lead to implementation of changes if the credibility of the simulation method is assured. This is achieved by ensuring each stage of the simulation project is undertaken correctly.

Organisational Context of Implementation

A simulation modelling project can use extensive resources both in terms of time and money. Although the use of simulation in the analysis of a one-off decision, such as investment appraisal, can make these costs low in terms of making the correct decision, the benefits of simulation can often be maximised by extending the use of the model over a period of time. It is thus important that, during the project proposal stage, elements are incorporated into the model and into the implementation plan that assist in enabling the model to provide ongoing decision support. Aspects include:

- Ensuring that simulation users are aware at the project proposal stage that the simulation is to be used for on-going decision support and will not be put to one side once the immediate objectives are met.
- Ensuring technical skills are transferred from simulation analysts to simulation users. This ensures understanding of how the simulation arrives at results and its potential for further use in related applications.

- • Ensuring communication and knowledge transfer from simulation consultants and industrial engineers to business managers and operational personnel. The needs of managerial and operational personnel are now discussed in more detail.

Managerial Involvement

The cost associated with a simulation project means that the decision of when and where to use the technique will usually be taken by senior management. Thus an understanding of the potential and limitations of the technique is required if correct implementation decisions are to be made. The Simulation Study Group (1991) found that 'there is a fear amongst UK managers of computerisation and this fear becomes even more pronounced when techniques that aid decision-making are involved'. This is combined with the fact that even those who do know how to use simulation become 'experts' within a technically oriented environment. This means that those running the business do not fully understand the technique which could impact on their decision to use the results of the study.

Operational Involvement

Personnel involved in the day-to-day operation of the decision area need to be involved in the simulation project for a number of reasons. They usually have a close knowledge of the operation of the process and thus can provide information regarding process logic, decision points and activity durations. Their involvement in validating the model is crucial in that any deviations from operational activities, seen from a managerial view, to the actual situation can be indicated. The use of process maps and a computer-animated simulation display both provide a means of providing a visual method of communication of how the whole process works (as opposed to the part certain personnel are involved in) and facilitates a team approach to problem solving by providing a forum for discussion.

Simulation can be used to develop involvement from the operational personnel in a number of areas. It can present an ideal opportunity to change from a top-down management culture and move to greater involvement from operational personnel in change projects. Simulation can also be a strong facilitator of communicating ideas up and down an organisation. Engineers for example can use simulation to communicate reasons for taking certain decisions to operational personnel who might suggest improvements. The use of simulation as a tool for employee involvement in the improvement process can be a vital part of an overall change strategy. The process orientation of simulation provides a tool for analysis of processes from a cross-functional as opposed to a departmental perspective. This is important because powerful political forces may need to be overcome in ensuring departmental power does not prevent change from a process perspective.

The choice of simulation software should also take into consideration ongoing use of the technique by personnel outside of the simulation technicians. For ongoing use software tools need to provide less complex model building tools. This suggests the use of visual interactive modelling tools which incorporate iconic model building and menu facilities, making this type of simulation more accessible. There is also a need for training in statistical techniques for valid experimentation analysis. In summary the following needs are indicated:

- Knowledge transfer from technical personnel to managerial and operational staff of the potential application of simulation.
- Training at managerial/operational levels in statistical techniques from companies and universities.
- Training at managerial/operational levels in model building techniques from companies and universities.
- Use of simulation as a communication tool between stakeholders in a change programme. The use of animation is useful.
- Use of suitable software, such as a visual interactive modelling system, to provide a platform for use by non-technical users.
- Incorporation of simulation in process change initiatives such as business process re-engineering (BPR).

Summary

In order that the results of the simulation are implemented, it is necessary to document the detail of the simulation study in a project report. The report should outline the role of simulation in providing support to any future implementation activities. Management understanding of the limitations of the simulation method is required so that support is forthcoming for implementation of simulation study results. Implementation also depends on the understanding and involvement of operational personnel who are affected by any changes.

194   *Simulation Modelling for Business*

Exercises

9.1. The simulation modeller needs to take into account the needs of management and operational personnel to ensure successful project implementation. What are these needs?

9.2. Discuss the advantages and disadvantages of employing a specialist simulation modeller or conducting simulation studies using end-user personnel.

Chapter 10

Case Studies

Andrew Greasley and Duncan Shaw

Introduction

This chapter provides a number of case study materials for tutors. The case studies are suitable for short courses, residential study, distance learning and undergraduate single semester modules. The case studies cover the areas of model development and presentation of results, experimentation with a pre-built model and use of a spreadsheet to examine the mechanics of the discrete-event method.

Case studies 1-5 are suitable for a two or three day course on simulation modelling. Students can work in groups on different case studies and build and present model results quickly.

Case 6 is a slightly more complex study which has been provided to students on a distance learning course in MSc Health Services Management and a weekend residential for an MSc in Manufacturing Management. The simulation is provided as a run-time version (written by the author in PASCAL) for students to undertake simulation experimentation.

Case 7 is used by undergraduate and postgraduate students in groups over a semester.

Case 8 is a spreadsheet based discrete-event simulation model which allows the discrete-event mechanism and statistical analysis techniques to be studied by students.

Case Study 1: A Petrol Station

Introduction

The management of a petrol filling station has noticed a steady increase in the flow of customers into the petrol station over recent months. This has led to an increase in queuing times at the (self-service) petrol pumps and at the payment counter.

The Process

Customers arrive at the petrol station and look to see if a petrol pump is available. If no pumps are available they drive away, otherwise they refill their vehicle with petrol. They then proceed to the payment till and proceed with the payment process. On entering the petrol station, customers queue at the first available pump.

The Objective

Currently there are four petrol pumps and one payment till. Management wishes to ensure that less than 12 cars drive away over an eight hour period. Also there is a requirement that the customer average waiting time is no more than five minutes at the till. How many pumps and payment tills are required to meet this objective?

Data

Customer arrival rate: exponential distribution with a mean of three minutes.
Pump service time: triangular distribution with a minimum of four minute, mean of six minutes, maximum of ten minutes.
Payment service time: triangular distribution with a minimum of one minute, mean of four minutes, maximum of six minutes.

Instructions

Build a model of the petrol station using simulation software. Run the simulation five times for 480 minutes and calculate the average number of customers that 'drive away' and the average queue time at the payment till. Determine how many pumps and payment tills are required to meet the objectives stated.

Case Study 2: A Coffee Shop

Introduction

The coffee shop sells a variety of hot beverages, soft and alcoholic drinks
and snacks. The customers can be categorised into two groups, those who
have a takeaway order and those who sit-in with their order. At present
both types of customer are served at a single location which is staffed by
two waiters. Management wishes to investigate the effect on waiting time if
a separate queue was provided for takeaway and sit-in service, each staffed
by one waiter.

The Process

Customers arrive at the coffee shop and wait in the queue for service.
Takeaway customers leave the shop immediately, whilst sit-in customers
take their order to a table.

The Objective

Currently there is one queue with two waiters. The aim is to predict the
effect of a move to a system of two queues, one for each type of service.

Data

Takeaway Customer arrival rate: exponential distribution with a mean of
three minutes. Sit-in Customer arrival rate: exponential distribution with a
mean of four minutes. Takeaway Customer Service Time: triangular
distribution with a minimum of one minute, mean of three minutes,
maximum of six minutes. Sit-in Customer service time: triangular
distribution with a minimum of 0.5 minutes, mean of two minutes,
maximum of five minutes.

Instructions

Build a model of the coffee shop using simulation software. Run the
simulation five times and calculate the average queue time at the service
location for each type of customer. Build a second model with a separate
queue for each type of customer. Run the simulation five times and
calculate the average queue time at the service location for each type of
customer. Which is the best system?

Case Study 3: A Supermarket

Introduction

A supermarket has a number of checkout tills in operation for its customers. Management has made a 'customer service promise' that if more than one person is in front of a customer at a checkout then another checkout will be opened for service.

The Process

Customers arrive at the supermarket, select their purchases and wait in a queue for service. Customers choose the smallest queue.

The Objective

Currently there are ten tills available throughout the day. Management wishes to predict the maximum amount of tills required at any one time if the new 'customer service promise' is put into operation.

Data

Customer arrival rate: exponential distribution with a mean of one minute. Customer service time: triangular distribution with a minimum of two minutes, mean of five minutes, maximum of 12 minutes.

Instructions

Build a model of the supermarket using simulation software. Run the simulation five times and calculate the maximum queue size at the ten tills. Build a second model with a policy of opening a new till. Run the simulation five times and note the maximum queue size at the tills. What is the maximum number of tills required using the new system?

Case Study 4: A Garage

Introduction

A garage undertakes the replacement of tyres and exhausts on motor vehicles. Customers arrive and expect replacement tyres or exhausts to be fitted while they wait. A service bay is dedicated to either tyre or exhaust replacement. Management wishes to determine the number of bays required to ensure that queue time does not exceed 15 minutes.

The Process

Customers arrive at the garage, and wait in a queue for either tyre or exhaust replacement. Customers leave after service.

The Objective

Management wishes to predict the maximum amount of service bays required to ensure that queue time does not exceed 15 minutes.

Data

Customer arrival rate: exponential distribution with a mean of five minutes. 40 per cent of customers require exhaust service, 60 per cent require tyre service. Customer service time: triangular distribution with a minimum of 15 minute, mean of 25 minutes, maximum of 45 minutes.

Instructions

Build a model of the garage using simulation software. Run the simulation five times and calculate the maximum queue time. How many bays are required to ensure that the queue time does not exceed 15 minutes?

Case Study 5: A Night Club

Introduction

A night club operates a system for entry where customers can either pay for a discounted ticket in advance or pay the full admission price on the door. At present both types of customers queue in the same line with two admission staff. Management wishes to investigate the possibility of using a separate queue for ticket and non-ticket entry and measure the average customer queue time.

The Process

Customers arrive at the night club, and wait in a queue. Ticket customers hand in their ticket and enter. Non-ticket customers pay for entry and enter.

The Objective

Management wishes to predict the effect of moving from a single queue to a two queue system.

Data

Ticket customer arrival rate: exponential distribution with a mean of three minutes. Non-ticket customer arrival rate: exponential distribution with a mean of five minutes. Ticket customer service time: triangular distribution with a minimum of 0.1 minutes, mean of 0.5 minutes, maximum of one minute. Non-ticket customer service time: triangular distribution with a minimum of one minute, mean of two minutes, maximum of four minutes.

Instructions

Build a model of the night club using simulation software. Run the simulation five times and calculate the maximum wait time. Change the queue system to a separate entry system for ticket and non-ticket customers. Run the simulation five times and calculate the maximum wait time.

Case Study 6: A Hospital Ward

The PASCAL Based Simulation System

The PASCAL based simulation system allows the creation of a run-time simulation program that students can run from a floppy disk and keep, without license restrictions. The computer simulation is produced using a simulation development tool based on the work of Davies and O'Keefe (1989) which provides PASCAL code for the three-phase, event scheduling and process methods of building simulation models. The simulation uses the three-phase version of the activity based approach. The tool has been constructed using the object oriented programming approach by the author and contains over 10000 lines of PASCAL code. The program consists of two elements: the 'RUNSIM' program provides the coding for the simulation logic; and 'SIMPAINT' provides drawing facilities for the simulation graphical background and animation icons. For each simulation the tutor draws the animation layout using the SIMPAINT program, codes the simulation logic in PASCAL and compiles the program to create a program the student can execute in WINDOWS. An executable version of the hospital ward simulation is available from the author (a.greasley@aston.ac.uk). An example of the hospital animation display is shown in figure 10.1.

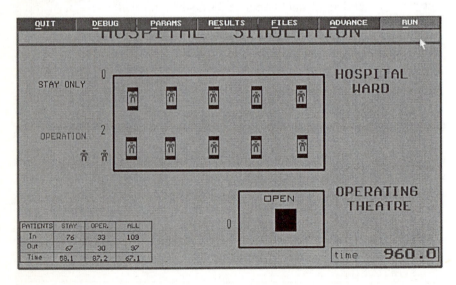

Figure 10.1 PASCAL hospital ward simulation display

Figure 10.2 shows the menu input screen which is specified by the tutor for each model. In this case the parameters for the hospital simulation are presented.

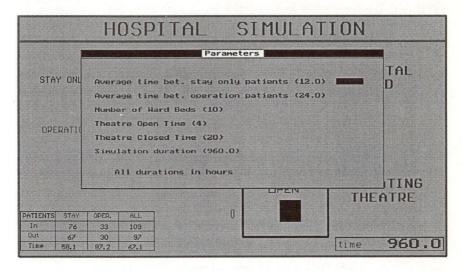

Figure 10.2 PASCAL hospital ward model input display

After each replication of the simulation the students can display the model results in a format specified by the tutor. Figure 10.3 shows the hospital ward results screen.

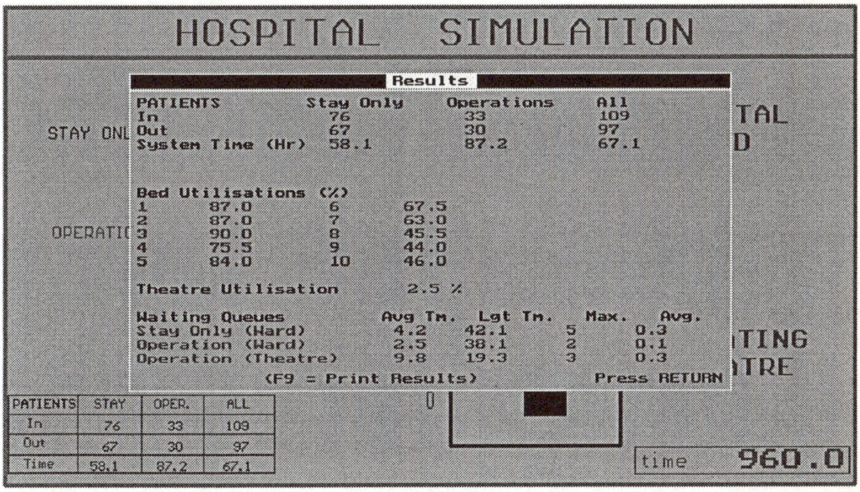

Figure 10.3 PASCAL hospital ward results screen display

Introduction

The purpose of the simulation is to examine the effect of different resource levels (e.g. the number of beds) on the service given to patients (measured by the length of the waiting list) while patients are admitted and, following treatment, discharged from a hospital ward.

The Process

Patients are classified into two types and go through the following stages:

Stay-Only Patients

  • Hospital ward stay-only

Operation Patients

  • Pre-Operative Stay in the Ward
  • Wait for the Operating Theatre (if not available)
  • Operation
  • Post-Operative Stay in the Ward

If both the stay-only and operation patients are waiting for a ward bed, stay-only patients are given preference.

The Objective

Management wishes to assess the average stay-only patient and average operation patient waiting list sizes with the bed ward provision set to eight, ten and 12 beds in turn.

Data

Stay-only patient arrival rate: exponential distribution with a mean of 0.5 hours. Operation patient arrival rate: exponential distribution with a mean of 1.5 hours. Time for stay-only stay: triangular distribution with a minimum of two hours, mean of 2.5 hours, maximum of three hours. Time for pre-op stay: triangular distribution with a minimum of 0.5 hours, mean of one hour, maximum of 1.5 hours. Time for post-op stay: triangular distribution with a minimum of 2.5 hours, mean of three hours, maximum of 3.5 hours. Operation duration: normal distribution with a mean of 0.75 hours, standard deviation of 0.25 hours. The operating theatre is open from 4.00am until 8.00pm. The simulation runs continuously for 960 hours before results are observed.

Instructions

The simulation is run for 10 times at each setting to obtain a range of results. Run the simulation for eight, ten and 12 bed provision and note the average waiting time for the hospital ward.

Case Study 7: A Factory Simulation

Introduction

The following is an outline of the factory process and information needed to build the simulation model.

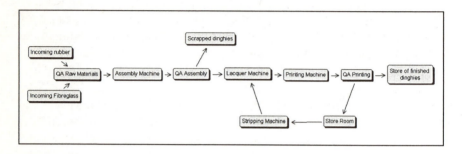

Figure 10.4 Diagram of the factory plant layout

To explain the diagram of the factory plant layout, raw materials in the form of rubber and fibreglass are delivered to the factory. These raw materials go through a short Quality Assurance Process (Raw Materials) before being loaded onto the Assembly Machine. The Assembly Machine cuts, shapes and glues all of the raw materials to build the dinghy. A finished waterproof dinghy comes out of the Assembly Machine. That dinghy then goes through a Quality Assurance Process (Assembly) where some are found to be so poorly constructed that they have to be scrapped (there is no selling price for these scrapped dinghies). The perfect dinghies continue on to the Lacquer Machine where a waterproof lacquer is applied. The dinghy then continues on to the Printing Machine where the company's branded transfers are applied. The dinghy goes through another Quality Assurance Process (Printing) where the quality of the lacquer and the application of the transfers are checked. If the dinghy fails at this stage then it goes into a Store Room and waits to be stripped down by the Stripping Machine where all the lacquer and transfers are removed. These dinghies then need to have the lacquer and transfers re-applied – but the priority for the Lacquer Machine is for those dinghies coming from the QA Assembly. If the dinghy passes this Quality Assurance Process (Printing) then it goes to the Store of Finished Goods where it waits to be delivered to the customer.

The Process

This piece of work was designed for students who are capable modellers and who wanted to experience the process of performing an entire simulation project. Students are split up into groups of about five people and typically have about six weeks to complete the project.

The modelling in this project is not extremely challenging because the focus is on managing and performing an entire simulation project from data collection to the presentation of results – not just on building a simulation model. Students are also required to cost the financial implications of their recommended factory configuration.

Students begin by preparing questions to ask the client (the Managing Director) about the factory to be simulated. However, the students never actually meet the client and instead are directed to the Operations Foreman who is very suspicious of the intentions behind the simulation project and so is not volunteering information. Instead the students will have to ask for all of it. The foreman will ask some tough questions of the students as to: what is their remit? why have they been brought in? what they think they will recommend? and whether they are going to recommend redundancies because that is what management consultants always do (!)? The information which the foreman will provide to students in the first meeting is detailed below.

Furthermore the foreman is not entirely honest with the students and prefers to tell them what he thinks they should hear rather than what the reality of the situation is. For example, the students might ask what is the target production per week for the factory. Currently the factory will produce about seven to nine dinghies per week, but the foreman will only tell them 20 dinghies, because is performance-related pay depends on the factory producing 20 dinghies per week. Also, the foreman will not tell the students about the Quality Assurance Process between the entry of materials and the Assembly machine.

The foreman will not volunteer information for the students. However it is important that students have all of the information to be able to build an initial simulation model.

At the second client meeting the students again meet with the foreman. The information the foreman will give the students in this second meeting is detailed below – the information coloured yellow is information which contradicts that which he gave them during their previous meeting. The students will demonstrate their model to the client. The client is still suspicious and so identifies many weaknesses in the model, for example, the icons representing machinery look nothing like the machinery on the shop-floor, the process times have changed, the breakdown times are wrong, the amount of manpower available has changed.

The foreman might not be patient with the students and will blame them for copying down his figures incorrectly. He might even go so far as to ask if using the wrong data was done in order to convince the Managing Director to sack people.

The foreman will look at the factory configuration and tell the students that they have missed out the Quality Assurance Process between the entry of materials and the Assembly machine.

The foreman will also tell students about any financial information they need. Students might ask about the amount of investment which the company are willing to provide. The foreman will say that the students should provide a business case for any investment they propose. Also he will say that the market for dinghies is buoyant and that they will easily be able to sell as many dinghies as they make. The foreman will say that the company has always had as its policy that they must make a 40 per cent return on the sale of all dinghies.

The written material provided to the students is shown on pages 209-210. The information given to students in their first meeting with the foreman is given on pages 211-212. The information given to students in their second meeting with the foreman (shaded information is that which has changed since the first meeting) is given on pages 213-214.

The Factory Simulation

The Situation

Dinghies Inc. has been trading for some 20 years. As its name suggests, Dinghies Inc. is a company which has developed expertise in the construction of dinghies. It has recently appointed a new management team (hereby referred to as 'the Team') to take the company to the leading edge in dinghy construction during the 21st Century.

The Team is keen to make a significant impact on the performance of the company in order to impress its shareholders. They see that one significant way of making this impact is through improving the operations of the company.

In order to make this improvement the Team are willing to make a small financial investment to improve the performance of their Dinghy Construction Unit (where the dinghies are assembled from a pile of parts). How much of a financial investment the Team are willing to make will depend on the justification they are given for the investment. Hence they have kept an open mind on what to invest in, and how much they will invest.

The Team recently advertised for consultancy assistance in order that they might learn more about the real problems in the Dinghy Construction Unit and how to solve those problems.

Your Role

You belong to a Consultancy Unit and are an expert in visual interactive simulation. You and your colleagues in 'The Consultancy Unit' have won a contract to assist Dinghies Inc. in the development of their awareness of their operations in the Dinghy Construction Unit. In your bid you claimed that you would:

- model and report on their existing operations using appropriate simulation software,
- explore the constraints under which their Dinghy Construction Unit operates,
- advise on where their intended financial investment would have the most impact on the operations of the Dinghy Construction Unit.

The Team are willing to provide information on their existing operations.

How You Should Proceed

The Team have arranged for you to meet with the Operations Foreman of the Dinghy Construction Unit. It is the foreman who will be able to provide you with the information that you need for your work.

You should meet up with the foreman and collect the information you will need to build your simulation model. Be warned, the foreman is not aware of simulation. He has no idea of what information you will need. You might benefit from meeting your Consultancy Unit before you meet the foreman so that you can decide on the questions to ask and who is going to ask them.

Financial Information

	£
Sales from Dinghies RRP	2000
Cost : Raw materials per dinghy	600
Cost : Overheads per dinghy	100
Cost : Machine Depreciation per dinghy	110
Cost : Labour per dinghy	140
Total Cost of Sales	950
Anticipated Profit per dinghy	1050

Labour Patterns

8	Hours a day
5	Days a week
14	Workers
£200	per worker per week
12.50%	Absentee Rate

No possibility of night shift

Order Batch Sizes

	Per dinghy	Batch size	Interarrival time
Rubber	100 kgs	500 kgs	2 times per wk (1200 mins)
Fibreglass	125 kgs	1000 kgs	1 time per wk (2400 mins)

Turn away raw material when we have 2.5 weeks in the store

Machine Information

	Cost New	MTTR (weeks)	MTBF (weeks)	Labour Required	Duration (mins)	MTTR (mins)	MTBF (mins)
				5 fitters/			
1 Assembly	40000	3	26	1 general	200	7200	62400
1 Lacquer	20000	2	26	3 fitters	50	4800	62400
1 Printing	15000	1	13	3 fitters	80	2400	31200
1 Stripping	35000	0.5	13	4 fitters	240	1200	31200
1 QA Assembly	0	0	0	2 general	15	0	0
1 QA Printing	0	0	0	2 general	25	0	0

Assumptions

Must make 40% profit per dinghy

Management says we must make 20 dinghies per week

Cost of borrowing money to buy a new machine, 15% (per annum pro rata)

Labour, 11 fitters, 3 general - general cannot do fitters job

Stripping machine always gets priority - no fitters take part from QA Assembly when there is one on Stripping, they wait and take it.

Financial Information

	£
Sales from Dinghies RRP	*2000*
Cost : Raw materials per dinghy	600
Cost : Overheads per dinghy	100
Cost : Machine Depreciation per dinghy	110
Cost : Labour per dinghy	140
Total Cost of Sales	*950*
Anticipated Profit per dinghy	**1050**

Labour Patterns

8 Hours a day
5 Days a week
14 Workers
£200 per worker per week.
10% Absentee Rate

Good possibility of night shift

Order Batch Sizes

	Per dinghy	Batch size	Interarrival time
Rubber	100 kgs	500 kgs	2 times per wk (1200 mins)
Fibreglass	125 kgs	1000 kgs	1 time per wk (2400 mins)

Turn away raw material when we have 2.5 weeks in the store
We never run out of stock as it is supplied within one day of our order.

Machine Information

	Cost New	MTTR (weeks)	MTBF (weeks)	Labour Required	Duration (mins)	MTTR (mins)	MTBF (mins)
1Assembly	40000	2	52	5 fitters/ 1 general	200	7200	62400
1Lacquer	20000	1	26	3 fitters	50	4800	62400
1Printing	15000	1	26	3 fitters	80	2400	31200
1Stripping	35000	0.5	13	4 fitters	240	1200	31200
1QA Materials	0	0	0	2 general	15	0	0
1QA Assembly	0	0	0	2 general	15	0	0
1QA Printing	0	0	0	2 general	25	0	0

Assumptions

Must make 40% profit per dinghy

Like to make 20 dinghies per week - personal PRP objective

Cost of borrowing money to buy a new machine 15% (per annum pro rata)

Labour, 11 fitters, 3 general - general cannot do fitters job
We have just trained all general staff to be fitters.

Stripping machine always gets priority - no fitters take part from QA Assembly when there is one on Stripping, they wait and take it.

Case Study 8: A Supermarket Simulation

Introduction

The following case provides an opportunity to introduce the discrete-event simulation technique to students on a platform they are familiar with, the spreadsheet. The simulation is implemented using the Visual Basic for Applications (VBA) programming language which is incorporated in the Microsoft EXCEL spreadsheet. The VBA coding for the spreadsheet is published in Greasley (1998) or can be obtained from the author on request (email: a.greasley@aston.ac.uk).

The Case Study

A small supermarket has four busy tills which process a mix of customers who use either a basket or trolley to carry goods. The supermarket manager wishes to increase income by attracting more custom from people 'dropping in' to purchase only a few items. He has noticed these customers are particularly sensitive to waiting time and will pay the higher prices at the corner shop if they have to wait too long. He considers allocating one of the four tills specifically for 'basket' customers ordering five or fewer items. He wishes to predict what improvement this change will have on the waiting time of basket customers and the overall effect on waiting time for all customers. He thus collects data on customer arrival rates and the time to process each customer at the till.

In terms of a discrete-event model the problem will be conceptualised as a mythical supermarket system in which an input stream of entities representing trolley and basket customers arrives to queue at one of the four tills present. Trolley customers are defined as customers carrying greater than five items. When a till is available the entity is delayed for the process time and then releases the till for further use.

Running the Simulation

The simulation is run by selecting the 'result' screen (figure 10.5) and clicking on the relevant RUN button to activate the required scenario. The first scenario is undertaken with all four tills available to basket and trolley customers. The second scenario makes till 1 unavailable to customers with over five items (i.e. trolley customers).

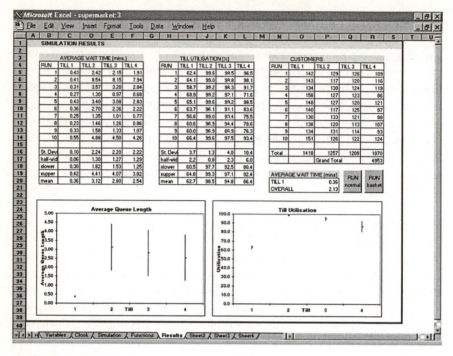

Figure 10.5 Spreadsheet simulation 'results' screen

Statistical Analysis

The results could be analysed with a spreadsheet package such as @RISK™ or Crystal Ball™ but in this case no previous knowledge of these facilities is assumed and so the statistical analysis is undertaken directly on the spreadsheet.

The supermarket simulation is treated as a terminating simulation with a duration of 480 minutes representing one eight hour day. No attempt is made to clear customers in the system at the end of this period in order to simplify coding. Because of the stochastic nature of the results, repeated runs are used to provide a sample from which to estimate the mean and compute a confidence interval or range that is likely to include the exact value of the mean. To form a confidence interval the average of the data points is found. Then a distance, or half-width, either side of this average is calculated and a risk or significance level which provides an indication of the confidence we can place in the measure is selected.

Results

The results of the supermarket simulation are displayed on the 'results' spreadsheet (figure 10.5). The average wait time, till utilisation and customers at each till are updated as each run is performed. The statistical figures are then calculated on the spreadsheet automatically and the graphs updated simultaneously. The hi-low graph type is used to show the mean and upper and lower limits for each recorded variable. The length of each graph tick provides a useful indication of the variability of the results. The results are summarised using the average wait time variable below:

Four Till Operation
Till 1 = 1.70 minutes average wait time
Overall = 1.40 minutes average wait time
One 'Basket' Till + Three Till Operation
Till 1 = 0.36 minutes average wait time
Overall = 2.13 minutes average wait time

Thus it can be seen that the provision of a 'basket' queue will reduce wait time and thus improve service quality for these customers. However this improvement does lead to an overall increase of wait time at all the tills. Further experiments could be undertaken by altering the input variables, such as the interarrival time, the number of items in a basket or trolley, or even the number of tills available. This is most conveniently implemented by allowing the user to alter the value of a variable from a spreadsheet cell. It is then a simple task to read the variable from the cell, using the VBA™ system, and use this as a parameter within the simulation model.

Discussion of Use

As an educational tool the statistical analysis displayed on the results screen can be used as an introduction to the kind of analysis required for the experimentation method and the results which can be produced from that analysis. Topics of discussion could include the need for replications, the use and choice of statistical analysis and the choice of performance indicators for the system being studied.

To help obtain a clearer understanding of the discrete-event method, the model can be operated in 'step' mode and students' attention directed to the simulation 'calendar' screen (figure 10.6). This displays bound event details of entities on the simulation calendar. Figure 10.6

actually shows the calendar just before the execution of entity number 34 for the 'choose till' event.

	A	B	C	D	E	F	G	H
1	ENTITY NUMBER	BOUND EVENT TIME	BOUND EVENT NUMBER	BOUND EVENT DESCRIPTION	SIMULATION TIME			
2	34	6.875	3	Choose Till	6.875			
3	21	6.900	4	Finished at Till 1				
4	31	7.000	50	Collect Statistics				
5	23	7.574	7	Finished at Till 4				
6	26	7.950	8	Trolley Arrival				
7	35	8.184	2	Basket Arrival				
8	18	12.386	6	Finished at Till 3				
9	13	15.893	5	Finished at Till 2				
10								
11								
12				Microsoft Excel				
13								
14				STEP MODE - press RETURN key to continue				
15								
16				OK				
17								
18								
19								
20								
21								
22								

Results \ calendar \ Sheet3 \ Sheet4 /

Figure 10.6 Spreadsheet simulation step mode

Note the simulation time has been set to the event time. Students can observe how entities are sorted and executed in time order on the calendar and see how the simulation time 'jumps' to the time of the next bound event to be executed. The students could also be directed to follow the life-history of a particular entity by noting each bound event action as it appears on the calendar display, thus introducing students to a useful validation tool utilised by simulation developers. It would be a simple matter to extend the model coding to allow the display of a chosen entity life-history if required.

Many decision-makers are conversant with the spreadsheet interface but not with the simulation technique. A demonstration model such as the 'supermarket' example could be used to show the need for and potential of the simulation method. For use as a decision-making tool however, it needs to be considered that the spreadsheet simulation system is most suited to relatively small-scale applications because of the relatively slow execution of VBA code. The absence of a high-level simulation language will slow model translation and the current lack of animation facilities makes the construction and validation of a larger model difficult.

Summary

This case study provides an example of a fully discrete-event simulation system implemented on a spreadsheet.

Although the simulation has limited capabilities as a decision-making tool in a business setting it can be used to introduce end-users to the discrete-event method on a familiar platform. The aim is that this will encourage the adoption of specialised simulation packages for commercial applications.

In an educational setting the spreadsheet simulation model can be used as a platform for teaching students the mechanics behind the discrete-event approach. The spreadsheet results screen provides a starting point for a discussion on experimentation issues such as the need for replications and the use of statistical analysis of results. The step mode in combination with the spreadsheet 'calendar' screen allows students to see the mechanics behind the event calendar for scheduling future events, which is fundamental to the discrete method.

Bibliography

Banks, J. and Gibson, R. (1998), 'Simulation Modelling: Some Programming Required', *IIE Solutions*, February, pp. 26-31.

Banks, J., Carson, J.S., Nelson, B.L. and Nicol, D.M. (2001), *Discrete-Event System Simulation*, Third Edition, Prentice-Hall Inc., New Jersey.

Black, K. (1992), *Business Statistics: An Introductory Course*, West Publishing Company, St. Paul.

Bocij, P.; Chaffey, D.; Greasley, A.; Hickie, S. (2003), *Business Information Systems: Technology, Development and Management for the e-business*, 2nd edition, Pearson Education Limited.

Cloud, D.J. and Rainey, L.B. (eds) (1998), *Applied Modeling and Simulation: An Integrated Approach to Development and Operation*, McGraw-Hill, New York.

Cochran, J.K., Mackulak, G.T. and Savory, P.A. (1995), 'Simulation Project Characteristics in Industrial Settings', *INTERFACES*, Vol. 25(4), pp. 104-113.

Davies, R. and O'Keefe, R. (1989), *Simulation Modelling with Pascal*, Prentice-Hall Inc., New Jersey.

Fishwick, P.A. (1995), *Simulation Model Design and Execution: Building Digital Worlds*, Prentice-Hall Inc., New Jersey.

Forrester, J.W. (1961), *Industrial Dynamics*, MIT Press, Cambridge, Mass.

Forrester, J.W. (1994), 'System Dynamics, Systems Thinking, and Soft OR', *System Dynamics Review*, Vol. 10 (2-3), pp. 245-256.

Gerbing, D.W. (1999), *Relevant Business Statistics: Using Microsoft Excel*, South-Western Publishing Co., Ohio.

Gogg, T.J. and Mott, J.R.A. (1992), *Improve Quality and Productivity with Simulation*, JMI Consulting Group.

Goodwin, J.S. and Franklin, S.G. (1994), 'The Beer Distribution Game: Using Simulation to Teach Systems Thinking', *Journal of Management Development*, Vol. 13 (8), pp. 7-15.

Greasley, A. (1996a), 'Using Computer Simulation for Line Balancing: A Manufacturing Case Study', *BPICS Control*, Vol. 29 (9), pp. 19-21.

Greasley, A. (1996b), 'The Use of Simulation Modelling in an Organisational Context', *Proceedings of the IASTED/ISMM International Conference on Modelling and Simulation*, April 25-27, IASTED.

Greasley, A. (1998), 'An Example of a Discrete-Event Simulation on a Spreadsheet', *SIMULATION*, Vol. 70(3), pp. 148-166.

Greasley, A. (1999a), 'Using Simulation Modelling in Manufacturing Process Design', *Engineering Management Journal*, Vol. 9(4), pp. 187-192.

Greasley, A. (1999b), *Operations Management in Business*, Nelson Thornes Ltd.

Greasley, A. (2000a), 'Using Simulation to Assess the Service Reliability of a Train Maintenance Depot', *Quality and Reliability Engineering International*, Vol. 16(3), pp. 221-228.

Greasley, A. (2000b), 'A Simulation Analysis of Arrest Costs', *Journal of the Operational Research Society*, Vol. 51, pp. 162-167.

Greasley, A. (2000c), 'A Simulation of a Valve Manufacturing Plant', *Proceedings of the 2000 Summer Computer Simulation Conference,* Society for Computer Simulation, San Diego, USA.

Greasley, A. (2001), 'Costing Police Custody Operations', *Policing: An International Journal of Police Strategies & Management*, Vol. 24 (2), pp. 216-227.

Greasley, A. (2003a), 'A Simulation of a Workflow Management System', *Work Study*, Vol. 52 (5), pp. 256-261.

Greasley, A. (2003b), 'Using Business Process Simulation within a Business Process Reengineering approach', *Business Process Management Journal*, Vol. 9 (4), pp. 408-420.

Greasley, A. (2003c), 'An evaluation of a computerised road traffic accident reporting system using simulation', *Business Process Management Journal*, accepted.

Greasley, A. (2003d), 'A simulation of a cladding and window production facility', *Manufacturing Engineer*, Vol. 82 (1), pp. 26-29.

Greasley, A. (2003e), 'A simulation of a large-scale snacks production facility', *Proceedings of the EUROMA/POMS conference*, Vol. II, pp. 591-600.

Greasley, A. (2003f), 'A simulation of a production planning system in a gas cylinder manufacturing plant', *Proceedings of the International Conference on Industrial Engineering and Production Management*, Porto, Portugal, May 26-28.

Greasley, A. (2003g), 'The Use of Data Envelopment Analysis and Simulation in Process Redesign', *Proceedings of the Summer Computer Simulation Conference*, pp. 531-535.

Greasley, A. and Barlow, S. (1998), 'Using Simulation Modelling for BPR: Resource Allocation in a Police Custody Process', *International Journal of Operations and Production Management*, Vol. 18 (9/10), pp. 978-988.

Hannon, B. and Ruth, M. (1994), *Dynamic Modelling*, Springer-Verlag, New York.

Hansen, G.A. (1997), *Automating Business Process Reengineering: Using the Power of Visual Simulation Strategies to Improve Performance and Profit*, Second Edition, Prentice-Hall Inc., New Jersey.

Harrington, H.J. and Tumay, K. (2000), *Simulation Modeling Methods: To Reduce Risks and Increase Performance*, McGraw-Hill, New York.

Hill, D.R.C. (1996), Object-Oriented Analysis and Simulation, Addison-Wesley Publishers Ltd., Harlow.

Hill, T. (2000), *Manufacturing Strategy: Text and Cases*, Second Edition, Palgrave Macmillan.

Hlupic, V. (2000), 'Simulation Software: A Survey of Academic and Industrial Users', *International Journal of Simulation*, Vol. 1 (1/2), pp. 1-11.

Kaplan, R.S. and Norton, D.P. (1996), *The Balanced Scorecard: Translating Strategy into Action*, HBS Press, Boston.

Kelton, W.D., Sadowski, R.P. and Sadowski, D.A. (2002), *Simulation with ARENA*, Second Edition, McGraw-Hill, Singapore.

Kim, D.H. and Senge, P.M. (1994), 'Putting Systems Thinking into Practice', *System Dynamics Review*, Vol. 10 (2-3), pp. 277-290.

Law, A.M. and Kelton, W.D. (2000), Simulation Modeling and Analysis, Third Edition, McGraw-Hill, Singapore.

Law, A.M., McComas, M.G. and Vincent, S.G. (1994), *The Crucial Role of Input Modeling in Successful Simulation Studies*, Industrial Engineering, July.

Levine, D.M., Berenson, M.L. and Stephan, D. (1997), *Statistics for Managers using Microsoft Excel*, Prentice-Hall Inc., New Jersey.

Martilla, J.A. and James, J.C. (1977), 'Importance-Performance Analysis', *Journal of Marketing*, January.

McHaney, R. (1991), *Computer Simulation: A Practical Perspective*, Academic Press Inc., London.

Melão, N. and Pidd, M. (2003) 'Use of business process simulation: A survey of practitioners', *Journal of the Operational Research Society*, Vol. 54, pp.2-10.

Muller, D.J. (1996), 'Simulation: "What to do with the Model afterward"', *Proceedings of the 1996 Winter Simulation Conference*, J.M. Charnes, D.J. Morrice, D.T. Brunner and J.J. Swain (eds), Society for Computer Simulation, San Diego.

Nance, R.E. (1995), 'Simulation Programming Languages: An Abridged History', *Proceedings of the 1995 Winter Simulation Conference*, C. Alexopoulos, K. Kang, W.R. Lilegdon and D. Goldsman (eds), pp. 1307-1313.

Oakshott, L. (1997), *Business Modelling and Simulation*, Pitman Publishing, London.

Pegden, C.D., Shannon, R.E. and Sadowski, R.P. (1995), *Introduction to Simulation Using SIMAN*, Second Edition, McGraw-Hill, Singapore.

Peppard, J. and Rowland, P. (1995), *The Essence of Business Process Re-engineering*, Prentice Hall, Hemel Hempstead.

Pidd, M. (1998), *Computer Simulation in Management Science*, Fourth Edition, John Wiley & Sons Ltd., Chichester.

Pidd, M. (2003), *Tools for Thinking: Modelling in Management Science*, Second Edition, John Wiley & Sons Ltd, Chichester.

Pidd, M. and Cassel, R.A. (2000), 'Taking Cues from Java: Featuring How Discrete Simulation and Java Can Light Up the Web', *IEEE Potentials*, February/March.

Porcaro, D. (1996), 'Simulation Modeling and DOE', *IIE Solutions*, September.

Profozich, D. (1998), *Managing Change with Business Process Simulation*, Prentice Hall Inc., New Jersey.

Richmond, B. and Peterson, S. (1994), *Stella II. An Introduction to Systems Thinking*, High Performance Systems Inc., Hanover, NH.

Robinson, S. (1994), *Successful Simulation: A Practical Approach to Simulation Projects*, McGraw-Hill, Berkshire.

Rohrer, M. and Banks, J. (1998), 'Required Skills of a Simulation Analyst', *IIE Solutions*, May, pp. 20-23.

Schriber, T.J. and Brunner, D.T. (2000), 'Inside Simulation Software: How it Works and Why it Matters', *Proceedings of the 2000 Winter Simulation Conference*, SCS.

Senge, P. (1990), *The Fifth Discipline: The Art & Practice of The Learning Organization*, Century Business.

Severance, F.L. (2001), *System Modeling and Simulation: An Introduction*, John Wiley & Sons Ltd, Chichester.

Simulation Study Group (1991), *Simulation in U.K. Manufacturing Industry*, R. Horrocks (ed.), The Management Consulting Group, University of Warwick Science Park.

Slack, N., Chambers, S., Harland, C., Harrison, A. and Johnston, R. (1998), *Operations Management*, Second Edition, Pitman Publishing, London.

Slack, N. and Lewis, M. (2002), *Operations Strategy*, Pearson Education Limited, Harlow.

Sprague, R.H. and Watson, H.J. (eds), (1993), *Decision Support Systems: Putting Theory into Practice*, Third Edition, Prentice-Hall Inc., New Jersey.

Stahl, I. (1995), 'New Product Development: When Discrete-Event Simulation is Preferable to System Dynamics', *Proceedings of the 1995 EUROSIM Conference*, F. Breitnecker and I. Husinsky (eds), Elsevier Science Publishers B.V., Netherlands, pp. 1089-1094.

Thesen, A. and Travis, L.E. (1992), *Simulation for Decision Making*, West Publishing Company, St. Paul.

Vennix, J.A.M. (1996), *Group Model Building: Facilitating Team Learning Using System Dynamics*, John Wiley & Sons Ltd, Chichester.

Watson, H.J. and Blackstone, J.H. (1989), *Computer Simulation*, Second Edition, John Wiley & Sons Ltd., Chichester.

Welch, P.D. (1983), *The Statistical Analysis of Simulation Results*, The Computer Performance Modeling Handbook, S.S. Lavenberg (ed.), Academic Press, New York.

Index

problem definition 37-38, 40
process mapping 23, 44, 52, 55
project implementation 37, 191
project presentation 190
project report 40, 190

random numbers 12, 46, 81, 139
replications 140
reports 3, 42
resource 15

scenarios 2, 4, 8-9, 12, 38-40, 133, 139
scheduling 8, 25, 41-42, 47
sensitivity analysis 37, 43, 45, 53, 75, 85
SIMAN 10, 25-26, 29, 134-136
SIMUL8 25, 29
simulation
    discrete-event 3, 11, 13, 15-16, 19-
        25, 52, 121, 133
    languages 10, 25-26, 55
software 2, 9-12, 15, 22-24, 26-32, 41,
        45, 81, 89, 132-133, 146
software 11, 23

sources of data 51
staff time 5, 24
steady-state 46, 143
strategic 10, 34, 36
structured walkthrough 132, 141
system dynamics 11, 13-15, 19

terminating systems 144
test runs 133, 141
trace analysis 133, 141
training 5, 22-24, 29-32, 38-39, 46
two-sample t-test 164

usage 34, 36-40, 46

variability 5-8, 23, 60-61, 84, 161
Visual Interactive Modelling (VIM) 4,
        25, 28, 129, 134
Visual Interactive Simulation (VIS) 3

warm-up 179
WITNESS 10, 25, 28-29